DELETED
FROM COLLECTION

1112 Montgomery Highway
Vestavia Hills, Alabama 35216

The
Chinese
Americans

By Barbara Lee Bloom

Lucent Books, 10911 Technology Place, San Diego, CA 92127

Other books in the Immigrants in America series:

The Cuban Americans
Primary Sources
The Russian Americans
The Vietnamese Americans

Library of Congress Cataloging-in-Publication Data

Bloom, Barbara Lee.
  The Chinese Americans / by Barbara Lee Bloom.
    p. cm. — (Immigrants in America)
Includes bibliographical references and index.
Summary: Discusses the diverse ethnicity of Chinese Americans, their immigration, social, cultural and political customs, employment, experiences with discrimination, and integration into American society.
  ISBN 1-56006-751-9 (alk. paper)
1. Chinese Americans—History—Juvenile literature. 2. Chinese Americans—Social conditions—Juvenile literature. 3. Immigrants—United States—Emigration and immigration—History—Juvenile literature. 5. United States—Emigration and immigration—History—Juvenile literature.
[1. Chinese Americans. 2. China—Emigration and immigration—History. 3. United States—Emigration and immigration—History.] I.Title. II. Series.
  E184.R9 G74 2002
  973'.049171—dc21

                                  2001003959

CONTENTS

FOREWORD

Immigrants have come to America at different times, for different reasons, and from many different places. They leave their homelands to escape religious and political persecution, poverty, war, famine, and countless other hardships. The journey is rarely easy. Sometimes, it entails a long and hazardous ocean voyage. Other times, it follows a circuitous route through refugee camps and foreign countries. At the turn of the twentieth century, for instance, Italian peasants, fleeing poverty, boarded steamships bound for New York, Boston, and other eastern seaports. And during the 1970s and 1980s, Vietnamese men, women, and children, victims of a devastating war, began arriving at refugee camps in Arkansas, Pennsylvania, Florida, and California, en route to establishing new lives in the United States.

Whatever the circumstances surrounding their departure, the immigrants' journey is always made more difficult by the knowledge that they leave behind family, friends, and a familiar way of life. Despite this, immigrants continue to come to America because, for many, the United States represents something they could not find at home: freedom and opportunity for themselves and their children.

No matter what their reasons for emigrating, where they have come from, or when they left, once here, nearly all immigrants face considerable challenges in adapting and making the United States

their new home. Language barriers, unfamiliar surroundings, and sometimes hostile neighbors make it difficult for immigrants to assimilate into American society. Some Vietnamese, for instance, could not read or write in their native tongue when they arrived in the United States. This heightened their struggle to communicate with employers who demanded they be literate in English, a language vastly different from their own. Likewise, Irish immigrant school children in Boston faced classmates who teased and belittled their lilting accent. Immigrants from Russia often felt isolated, having settled in areas of the United States where they had no access to traditional Russian foods. Similarly, Italian families, used to certain wines and spices, rarely shopped or traveled outside of New York's Little Italy, a self-contained community cut off from the rest of the city.

Even when first-generation immigrants do successfully settle into life in the United States, their children, born in America, often have different values and are influenced more by their country of birth than their parents' traditions. Children want to be a part of the American culture and usually welcome American ideals, beliefs, and styles. As they become more Americanized—adopting western dating habits and fashions, for instance—they tend to cast aside or even actively reject the traditions embraced by their parents. Assimilation, then, often becomes an ideological dispute that creates conflict among immigrants of every ethnicity. Whether Chinese, Italian, Russian, or Vietnamese, young people battle their elders for respect, individuality, and freedom, issues that often would not have come up in their homeland. And no matter how tightly the first generations hold onto their traditions, in the end, it is usually the young people who decide what to keep and what to discard.

The Immigrants in America series fully examines the immigrant experience. Each book in the series discusses why the im-migrants left their homeland, what the journey to America was like, what they experienced when they arrived, and the challenges of assimilation. Each volume includes discussion of triumph and tragedy, contributions and influences, history and the future. Fully documented primary and secondary source quotations enliven the text. Sidebars highlight interesting events and personalities. Annotated bibliographies offer ideas for additional research. Each book in this dynamic series provides students with a wealth of information as well as launching points for further discussion.

Chinese Immigration

The Chinese were some of the earliest immigrants to reach America. During the mid-1800s, because much of China was stricken with extreme poverty, men began leaving China seeking jobs. Although these men loved their homeland and families, they left both behind to sail thousands of miles across the Pacific Ocean to California or Hawaii in search of jobs or riches.

Gold Mountain

The early immigrants had every intention of returning to China with enough wealth to help their families and to live out their lives in the land of their ancestors. Because these men planned on returning home, they were known in their villages as sojourners, or temporary travelers. In 1849, though, tales of abundant gold in California, soon called Gold Mountain, reached the regions of China located on the South China Sea. By 1852, thousands of sojourners had set sail to seek their fortune.

Families in China became dependent on the money that the sojourners sent back, so the men overseas kept working year after year after year. Some became prospectors and miners throughout the West, following discoveries of gold and silver. Others found work on the fast-growing frontier. They became fishermen and helped establish commercial fishing along the West Coast. They cut timber in forests; they labored in early industries; they dug coal; they made swampland into farmland. When the transcontinental railroad was built, Chinese immigrants laid tracks through some of the most rugged land in America. Furthermore, their knowledge of the soil, plants, and cultivation and their willingness to labor long hours in the fields, vineyards, and orchards made the West one of the most productive agricultural regions in the nation. The Chinese immigrants' legacy in agriculture continues to this day.

Despite these contributions, Chinese immigrants faced an inconsistent welcome in America. As the Western states grew and prospered, the immigrants' labor and skill benefited the expansion of the frontier. However, when jobs and money became scarce, they were told to go back to China, and few new immigrants were allowed to come. Although the Chinese were some of the first immigrants to arrive, they were also the first to be excluded by specific laws.

Many of the first immigrants to the United States were Chinese men who came to California during the mid–nineteenth century in search of gold and silver.

Sandalwood Hills

Chinese immigrants also went to Hawaii, or Sandalwood Hills as they called it. During the mid-1800s, the islands were part of the Kingdom of Hawaii, which was ruled by a royal family of Hawaiians. Hawaii was green and lush, and Americans living on the islands wanted to use the land to grow sugar to make them rich. By 1900, American businessmen had made Hawaii a U.S. territory. More than half a century later, in 1954, Hawaii was admitted to full statehood.

During the 1850s, the lure of Hawaii for the Chinese was the promise of jobs. They arrived mostly as workers for sugar and rice plantations, and the state's agriculture flourished with their tending. During the late nineteenth century as Chinese immigrants on the mainland were shunned, on the islands they were welcomed for their labor, and their families fit in well among the Hawaiians. They helped boost Hawaii's production of pineapples and sugarcane and made the islands a place of wide cultural diversity.

These early immigrants to Hawaii and to the U.S. mainland were part of the first wave of Chinese immigrants. Some of them returned to China, but many settled down and eventually became American citizens.

Another Wave of Immigrants

Another wave of Chinese immigrants arrived in America after World War II. The Second World War and a civil war in China prompted this new influx of immigrants. These Chinese newcomers were different from the frontiersmen. Men, women, and even families came. They arrived from a variety of places—the People's Republic of China, the British colony of Hong Kong, and Taiwan—and they spoke a different Chinese dialect than the first wave spoke.

Most of the newer immigrants had lived in cities, and many were well educated; often, they had professional skills. Some became scientists, researchers, politicians, mathematicians, doctors, teachers, laborers, and computer experts. Again, their skills helped America prosper, and again they faced discrimination. Despite this, they settled in every section of the country. Today, Americans of Chinese ancestry can be found from New York to California to Georgia and Michigan.

CHAPTER ONE

Immigration Begins from Imperial China

For hundreds of years, Chinese rulers considered their vast empire the only civilized place in the world. By 214 B.C., the Chinese had built the Great Wall along China's western border to keep out "barbarians" (non-Chinese). To the east, they were protected by thousands of miles of ocean. As a result, most Chinese knew little about what happened beyond their own shores, and fewer still cared. The Chinese remained isolated this way for centuries, with only occasional Europeans venturing into their lands.

From the sixteenth to the nineteenth century, though, colonial powers from Europe made attempts to trade with China. These efforts to establish commerce and diplomatic relations were rejected by the Chinese emperors, but the foreigners were determined to change that policy by force of arms if necessary. The Chinese lost the battles that followed, and the colonial powers forced the Chinese government to allow Europeans into the country. Ultimately, the entrance of these powers into China had a profound impact on the nation.

In the eyes of some Chinese, losing battles with foreigners meant that their government had grown weak. Others resented the corruption and power of the imperial court. In response, peasants revolted. However, these uprisings only weakened the government and country further. In addition, the fighting, whether against the colonial powers or the Chinese rebels, often destroyed farms and villages in the region near the South China Sea.

Guangdong Province

The people of Guangdong (Kwangtung) province originated from pioneering tribes who moved southward as China's borders expanded. When they reached the South China Sea, they stopped traveling and established villages. Up until the nineteenth century, the rhythm of life in Guangdong remained almost unchanged. The people of this region spoke unique Cantonese dialects of Chinese. Most farmed the valleys; others planted crops on the terraced mountainsides; and fishermen caught fish and "farmed" the salt from the sea.

Here, as in all of China, the Chinese followed the teachings of Confucius, an ancient sage who preached respect for honest rulers, elders, and family. According to Confucianism, everyone from the poorest peasant to the emperor had a well-defined place in society. Farmers and laborers were held in higher esteem than merchants, and scholars were valued above all others. It was the duty of each son to look out for the well-being of his parents, and once a young man married, his wife, too, had an obligation to her husband's parents. Thus, for peasants in Guangdong, life centered around a large extended family, or clan, that made up an entire village. And because family was so important to the Chinese, they wrote their last name (their family's name) before their first.

Lee Chew, who later immigrated to the United States, described this family-centered life. In his childhood community,

> All the village belonged to the tribe [family] of Lee. They did not intermarry with one another, but the men went to other villages for their wives and brought them home to their fathers' houses, and men from other villages . . . chose wives from among our girls. . . .
>
> [In this community, most people grow rice and food crops but have houses away from the wet, insect-inhabited fields.] All the men of the village have farms, but they don't live on them. . . . They live in the village, but go out during the day time and work their farms, coming home before dark.[1]

Sometimes women also worked in the fields, but in general, it was their job to manage the home, cook, look after the needs of their children, and follow the wishes of their elders and husband.

Guangdong remained a quiet rural province until the sixteenth century when Spanish, Dutch, Portuguese, and British merchants began arriving eager to trade for Chinese goods such as spices, porcelain, silk, and tea. Once the Chinese saw and became enamored with the European luxuries, the imperial government seemed helpless to stop its subjects from trading with the barbarians. Moreover, many men left their villages, becoming seamen on foreign vessels and emigrating overseas in search of wealth. One young man recalled,

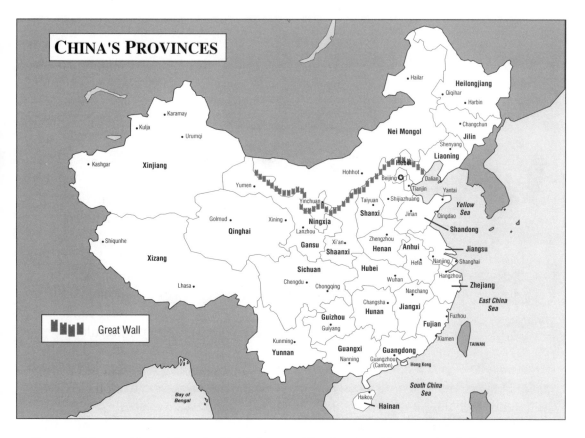

CHINA'S PROVINCES

Great Wall

Some of these things [that the British had] were very wonderful, enabling the red haired savages [the British] to talk [by telegraph] with one another, though they might be thousands of miles apart. They had suns [gas lights] that made darkness like day, and their ships carried earthquakes and volcanoes [cannons] to fight for them, and thousands of demons that lived in iron and steel houses [factories with steam engines and machines] spun their cotton and silk, pushed their boats . . . and did other work for them. They were constantly showing disrespect for their ancestors by getting new things to take the place of the old.[2]

Yet despite this perceived disrespect, many Chinese remained fascinated with life overseas and the opportunities that it seemed to offer.

Contact with Outsiders Increases

China's government disliked having its civilization contaminated by foreigners and their ideas. To keep its subjects at home, the Chinese government made emigration from China and contact with other countries a crime. As political scientist Kil Young Zo explains,

The official attitude toward the emigrants was outright hostility, regarding

A nineteenth-century Chinese painting shows foreign factories and trading stations in Canton harbor, which Emperor Qian Long opened for international trade in 1757.

all those who disappeared into, or appeared from, "lands beyond the sea," as potential rebels. An imperial edict of 1712 . . . declared that: "The Chinese government shall request foreign governments to have those Chinese who have been abroad repatriated [sent back to China] so they may be executed."[3]

Foreign governments, though, paid no attention to the edict and made no attempt to send immigrants back to China. In fact, European countries became more desirous of Chinese goods and more insistent with the passing years that China open itself to trade. As early as 1557, the Portuguese had established a fortified trading post at Macao, an island off the coast of Guangdong. By the eighteenth century, other colonial powers came from Europe, and it became obvious they would use any means

possible, even force if necessary, to take what they wanted. So in 1757, Chinese emperor Qian Long was coerced into opening the port of Canton, the capital of the province, for international trade.

The result was an influx of Europeans and their ideas. Traders, merchants, and Western missionaries entered China. According to historian John King Fairbanks,

St. Francis Xavier, one of the founders of the Jesuit order . . . died off the coast of China in 1552. During the next two centuries he was followed in the effort to Christianize China by some 463 selected and highly trained evangelists. . . . The great Jesuit pioneer Matteo . . . took twenty years to work his way step by step from the Portuguese community at Macao to the [imperial] court at Peking [Beijing].[4]

As missionaries brought Christianity, trade with Europeans brought prosperity to the region. Farmers learned to grow new vegetables from abroad such as sweet potatoes and yams, which thrived in the mild climate of southern China. The nation's merchants and tradesmen discovered new markets for Chinese goods, and craftsmen found new buyers for their wares. With new prosperity flowing into the region, the population steadily grew.

The growth in population, though, soon became a burden. Peasant farmers divided up their land among their sons until, by the nineteenth century, many plots had become too small to support a family. Furthermore, Guangdong was a tropical region where monsoon rains often led to disastrous floods. During the few dry years, drought killed almost all the crops, creating food shortages throughout the overpopulated province.

The Opium War

More than just small farms and insufficient food brought misery to the people of Guangdong. The outbreak of war added to the hardships of the peasants. The cause of the conflict was opium, an addicting drug that the British hoped to exchange for Chinese goods. The Chinese government imposed high tariffs on British goods to keep them out, but English merchants smuggled in opium, which they acquired from their colony in India. The emperor quickly saw how opium's addicting potential could destroy the productivity of his subjects; as the Chinese used opium, they got addicted and were less able to concentrate on their jobs,

farms, and families. The importation of the drug was ultimately banned by a decree from the emperor, but the British defied the decree, continuing to smuggle in opium.

A confrontation soon followed. The emperor sent a commissioner, a representative of the imperial court, to Canton. The commissioner went to the docks, ordered the opium chests removed, and demanded the drug be burned. Then he had the ashes floated on the river as an offering to the deities. Angry at the loss of the valuable cargo, England retaliated, using their guns and military might to defeat China in the First Opium War, lasting from 1839 to 1842. The Second Opium War involved the French as well as the British and ended in 1857.

The treaties signed after these wars forced China to open five of its ports to foreign trade, and to cede the island of

The English bombard Canton during the First Opium War.

Hong Kong to the British. England also demanded that China render monetary compensation for the damages to English ships and property caused during the war. In turn, to cover payments to the British, the imperial government raised taxes on the land. It fell to the people of Guangdong, on whose soil the war had been fought, to pay about 70 percent of the reparations for the First Opium War. Furthermore, the opium, which the British were now free to import to China, drained currency away from the province; profits went to English rather than Chinese merchants. This made prices on purchased goods rise, and everything became more expensive than before.

As making a daily living grew more difficult in Guangdong, most Chinese resented what they thought were the Europeans' attempts to weaken China and colonize their lands. Lee Chew remembers,

My grandfather told how the English foreign devils had made wicked war

The Manchus and the Taiping Rebellion

After thousands of years of rule by the Han (the native Chinese), in 1644 northern Manchu nomads conquered China and established the Qing dynasty. At first the dynasty prospered, but by the mid–nineteenth century the rulers had grown corrupt and were unable to rule efficiently. For some years the dynasty continued to rule, but the First Opium War brought a humiliating defeat to the empire and the Manchu army in 1842; the Europeans now demanded that China allow them to trade tea and opium within its borders.

The defeat dealt Chinese pride and patriotism a terrible blow. In the south, with its traditionally rebellious clans, secret anti-Manchu societies arose to force the Manchu rulers from China. One of the secret societies was called the Taiping Tienkuo (the Heavenly Kingdom of Great Peace).

Using the hatred for the conquering Manchu dynasty and his own version of Christianity, Hong Xiuquan, a peasant rebel, led men, women, and children on a crusade to save China. Hong Xiuquan's followers provided food, money, and weapons, and they were his troops as they fought the government soldiers in a conflict that became known as the Taiping Rebellion.

The imperial forces sent to do battle were a vicious group who raped, robbed, and burned out the peasants, driving even more farmers into the Taiping camp. Hong and his followers put up a good fight, winning many battles and bringing several villages and towns under their control. Despite these victories, the government's superior ammunition and resources prevailed in the end. Hong and the peasants were defeated, and the Manchu dynasty ruled China until 1911.

on the Emperor, and . . . had defeated his armies and forced him to admit their opium, so that the Chinese might smoke and become weakened and the foreign devils might rob them of their land.[5]

The evils of the foreigners were well recognized by the Chinese. Most believed that the Europeans, with what the Chinese thought were enchantments and spells, would take away their land and bring death to the people. As Fairbanks explains,

> In the Chinese view, the Western barbarians were outlandish in their physical characteristics, generally uncouth and smelling of mutton [sheep] fat. In slang they have been called "foreign devils" (fan-kuie or yang-kuei-tze), "big noses" (ta-pi-tzu), or "hairy ones" (mao-tzu). The official history . . . had described in some detail the Portuguese method of boiling and eating little Chinese children. Nineteenth century mission orphanages were thought to make medicine out of children's eyes and hearts. [So great was their fear that] peasant mothers used to shield their babies from a foreigner's unlucky glance and especially the black magic of his camera.[6]

The Taiping Rebellion and Clan Wars

Although some Chinese believed that their troubles were because of the evil foreigners, others blamed their own government and the corruption that had befallen

The dead bodies of rebel fighters in the aftermath of the Taiping Rebellion.

Manchu leaders of the Qing dynasty. After the First Opium War, discontent with the government increased, and peasants revolted against the imperial court in 1851. Demanding reform, Hong Xiuquan, a farmer, led rebels in an uprising against the Qing dynasty. Known as the Taiping Rebellion, the fighting lasted thirteen years before the emperor's troops finally subdued the rebels. The peasants, though, had almost succeeded in overthrowing the government and, in doing so, had greatly weakened the emperor's authority.

In addition to the battles of the Taiping Rebellion, local clan wars broke out and made life miserable in Guangdong. Because of the fighting, many families found their homes and villages lying in ruins and their crops burned, and they became desperate. In the face of such desperate circumstances, men anxious to support their

Sojourners Return

After only a few years in the United States, a few sojourners returned to China to live as men of great wealth. They became proof that success awaited those willing to seize the chance. In Hamilton Holt's book The Life Stories of Undistinguished Americans as Told by Themselves, *immigrant Lee Chew remembers one such man.*

[W]hen] I was about sixteen years of age, . . . a man of our tribe [village] came back from America and took ground as large as four city blocks and made a paradise of it. He put a large stone wall around and led some streams through and built a palace and summer house and about twenty other structures, with beautiful bridges over the streams and walks and roads. Trees and flowers, singing birds, water fowl and curious animals were within the walls.

The man had gone away from our village a poor boy. Now he returned with unlimited wealth, which he had obtained in the country of the American wizards. After many amazing adventures he had become a merchant in a city called Mott Street [New York City], so it was said.

When his palace and grounds were completed he gave a dinner to all the people who assembled to be his guests. One hundred pigs roasted whole were served on the tables, with chickens, ducks, geese and such an abundance of dainties [specialty foods such as dumplings, duck eggs, and pickled ginger] that our villagers even now lick their fingers when they think of it. He had the best actors from Hong Kong performing, and every musician for miles around was playing and singing. At night the blaze of the lanterns could be seen for many miles.

Having made his wealth among the barbarians [Americans] this man had faithfully returned to pour it out among his tribesmen.

families began to leave on ships from Canton, Hong Kong, and Macao in search of work abroad. The emigrants planned to stay away only three to five years and then return home with enough money to rebuild their homes and lead prosperous lives. These men became known in their villages as sojourners, or temporary residents, for none of them imagined they would stay away from China forever.

The Call of Foreign Lands

By the mid–nineteenth century, sojourners had several destinations to choose from. In 1841, a Chinese scholar named Wei Yun had written *The Geography of the World,* a series of books that told a great deal about the territories and nations beyond China's borders. Many Chinese were now curious about the people in other places and how they lived; Wei's descriptions excited them. He told of northern Mexico and California, calling these places golden lands with an abundance of birds and animals. Farmers there, Wei wrote, had thousands of sheep and cows. For many Chinese, this region seemed like a place where a hardworking man could succeed. Historian Liping Zhu writes,

> [California was] a wonderland with plenty of water, timber and honey. To most Chinese, particularly those living in the crowded southeastern part of the country, the abundance of natural resources in California and Mexico seemed almost beyond imagination.[7]

For others, Hawaii, or the Sandalwood Hills as they called it, held promise. During the 1830s, wealthy Americans living on the islands came to believe that huge profits could be made growing sugarcane and selling sugar to the United States. To grow sugarcane, though, plantation owners needed laborers to work in the cane fields. Hawaii itself had an inadequate supply, so planters looked to China, for the Chinese were known for their hard work and ability to tend crops. In Guangdong, the call for workers found many who were eager to listen.

Gold in California!

As Chinese men considered going abroad as a means of finding employment and earning money to help their families, tales of fabulous riches to be made in California reached them. Anthropologist Mary Coolidge explains, "The news of the dis-

covery of gold in the Sacramento Valley [California] in January, 1848, reached Hong Kong in the spring and created much excitement there."[8]

With the discovery of gold and the desire of many to reach the goldfields of California, ship captains saw the chance to make a lot of money by charging high prices for passage. They used any means they could to lure young men to their ships. As Coolidge writes,

> Masters of foreign vessels afforded every facility to emigration, distributing placards, maps and pamphlets with highly colored accounts of the Golden Hills, and reaping enormous profits as the demand for passages and freight increased. In 1850 forty-four

Chinese men listen to a Sunday service on board a ship bound for California.

vessels left Hong Kong for California with nearly 500 passengers and by the end of 1851 it was estimated that there were 25,000 Chinese in California engaged either in . . . mining or in domestic and manual labor.[9]

Leaving Home

Despite the tales of riches to be made abroad, the decision to leave China was often a hard choice. During the 1840s, life in the United States was unknown to most Chinese. Almost no one in China knew for certain what lay across the sea. Men worried about leaving their wives and families behind, and few could be sure when or if they would return.

Even though they faced the unknown, as more tales circulated about California, daring young men saw opportunity awaiting them abroad. Sociologist Betty Lee Sung tells of one sojourner, Chin Fatt Hing, whose "story is typical of the pioneer Chinese, many who came with him and many who came after him."

As a lad of nineteen, Fatt Hing had already seen and heard and learned more about the world than most of the men in his village. . . . For Fatt Hing was a fish peddler who went frequently from Toishan to Kawanghai [Chinese regions] on the [South China] coast to buy his fish to sell at market. . . .

One morning there was a great deal of commotion and excitement on the wharves. Elbowing his way to the center of the crowd, Fatt Hing caught snatches of the cause of the commotion [wild stories of gold] amidst the shouting and the pushing. . . .

In the gray dawn of early mornings following, Fatt Hing's ears strained to catch every word pertaining to the Mountain of Gold [California] on the wharves. His mind was already made up. . . .

He confided in no one for he did not wish to alarm his parents. True, they were not solely dependent upon him for support. He had two older brothers, but his parents would forbid him to go and he did not want to upset them. . . . [But at last he got his wish and was able to] persuade his parents to let him go. By that time, reports were filtering back that Mountain of Gold was no myth and that the gold was free to any who would come and mine. Then there was no holding Fatt Hing back.[10]

CHAPTER TWO

The Journey

lthough poverty and wars in China drove men to seek opportunity in America, before they began their travels, they needed to raise money for passage. Immigrants desperate to escape China used any means they could to secure a ticket on a sailing vessel. Once at sea, the seven-thousand-mile trip across the Pacific Ocean was a long and difficult journey. The travelers often faced heavy storms and high waves. Belowdecks they were jostled and tossed about, and many suffered from seasickness. Even if the weather was fair, they were packed into overcrowded quarters with squalid conditions.

Booking Passage Abroad

Once men decided to emigrate, they faced many obstacles. The first difficulty was how to get away. During the 1840s and 1850s, the Chinese emperor still considered it a crime to leave the country; he wanted all his subjects to remain under his rule. Those who were caught trying to leave China would be beheaded. So, men who wanted to leave had to find a way to get on board ship without being caught by officers of the imperial court.

Another obstacle to emigration from China was actually buying a ticket on a ship sailing to America. Booking passage was expensive for poverty-stricken Chinese, and immigrants used whatever methods they could find to raise the funds. The easiest was to collect money from family and friends. Sometimes parents even sold valued possessions to pay a son's fare.

If relatives had already reached America, they could help too. Reverend Otis Gibson, a missionary living among the Chinese, explained in 1887,

> Take a family of four or five boys and an old man. They hear stories about this country [America], and the ease with which money is quickly made. They get their earnings together and send one of the boys. He comes here [to California] and sends money back as fast as he can send it [to help his relatives move to America]. I think half the people come that way.[11]

Men without any money or family assistance could get a ticket to California by contracting for a loan from a Chinese or Western company. The "credit ticket" system, as this was called, allowed immigrants to borrow the money for their ticket and pay it off once they got to California. The companies often cheated the men, though, charging more than twice the cost of the original $40 ticket. In the beginning, the company that made the loan also found work for the man when he arrived in San Francisco. This made it easy to be sure the loan was repaid.

Most immigrants to Hawaii, on the other hand, became "contract laborers." Brokers for the sugar and rice plantation owners paid laborers' passage to the islands after the men signed a contract to work for an island planter for at least three years at set wages.

Leaving the Village

Once they had their ticket in hand, emigrants had to be careful about how they left China. Men generally started their journey by traveling on foot or in small boats from their villages to port cities like Hong Kong or Canton. But once there, if a man were caught boarding a foreign ship, he could face death.

Chin Fatt Hing was a young man who witnessed firsthand the dangers of being caught leaving China. As author Betty Lee Sung describes,

> [Chin Fatt Hing] was cautious. He confided in no one. . . . By the time Fatt Hing had gathered enough information to learn that he could buy passage on one of the huge foreign ships, he was shocked into a cold sweat to discover that the magistrate's soldiers had arrested many of the less discreet [young men] who had tried to board a ship. Belatedly, they had learned that it was a crime punishable by capital punishment [death] for a subject of the Emperor to emigrate from his homeland.

> Many more months of cautious probing rewarded Fatt Hing with the knowledge that the garrison [troop] leader could be bribed. . . . His father sold the water buffalo and Fatt Hing's mother pawned her earrings for his passage. Together they bade their son

a tearful farewell, and he was smuggled on board a Spanish ship bound for California.[12]

After the Second Opium War, Emperor Xianfeng, realizing he could no longer isolate China from the rest of the world, signed a series of treaties with foreign powers. As a result, in 1860, the imperial government relaxed its position on emigration, and those leaving the country could stay openly in *gam sam jong* (dormitories) provided by the labor broker or with relatives or friends.

Crossing the Pacific Ocean

Because so many men were eager to cross the Pacific, they were willing to make do with any accommodations. Shipmasters took advantage of that willingness. The sailing ships crossing the Pacific during the mid-1800s were originally built as cargo ships. Few passenger quarters existed on board, so the immigrants crowded into steerage, the cheap space where freight had previously been stored.

Belowdecks the accommodations were terrible. "Each person had a tiny bunk

French and Chinese officials sign a treaty in 1858, opening up commerce between the two countries. Such treaties paved the way for the Chinese government to relax its position on emigration.

measuring fifteen inches by six feet," explains historian Liping Zhu.

Only on a good day did the captain allow a small number of Chinese to come up on deck. During heavy winds and waves, the Chinese remained in the hold [belowdecks] with almost no light. Their food consisted of turnips, cabbage, bamboo shoots, dried fish, and rice cooked in water with some pork fat. Water was scarce. . . . Limited water, little sanitation, and decomposing vegetables all contributed to illnesses such as scurvy, diarrhea and food poisoning, which took a heavy toll of lives.[13]

Even those who remained healthy had a difficult journey. Of Chin Fatt Hing, one author writes,

After he was secreted on board, Fatt Hing discovered to his surprise that the entire hold was filled with young men like himself. They slept, sat, ate and waited on the straw mats on the floor. The air in the hold was stifling and foul, putrid from the vomiting of those who had not acquired their sea legs. Most of the time, the wind-swept decks were much too cold for the thin cotton or flax garments which Fatt Hing and his fellow passengers wore. Besides . . . Fatt Hing spent many days and nights with his nose pressed against a crack in the board covering the hold. Those days and nights were given to a lot of thinking with misgivings about the step that he had taken.[14]

In an attempt to calm their fears, immigrants tried to connect with each other, looking for neighbors, friends, even people with the same last name. It was important to know they belonged to some group. The Chinese assumed that a person with the name Chin or Lee or Wong would be related to another Chin or Lee or Wong. No matter how many generations back, they shared a common ancestor, and men soon formed strong bonds of friendship, taking care of one another in times of sickness and sorrow.

Pacific Mail Steamship Company

After 1868, conditions on board improved as steamships replaced sailing vessels crossing the Pacific Ocean. From then on, most immigrants to America traveled on ships owned by the Pacific Mail Steamship Company. Originally, this company had been commissioned by the U.S. Congress to carry mail from the Atlantic coast to Oregon Territory, but during the 1860s the U.S. Post Office added a line between San Francisco and Hong Kong. On these ships, the trip was more bearable, and the faster engines shortened the journey, which could last up to three months on sailing ships, by a couple weeks. During its first decade in operation, the Pacific Mail Steamship Company carried more than 124,000 Chinese sojourners back and forth across the Pacific Ocean.

Most of the poor peasants still journeyed in the steerage section, but food and sanitation improved on the swifter steamships. Conditions in this class continued to be

Chinese immigrants, aboard a Pacific Mail steamship in 1876, enjoy a meal prepared by a Chinese cook during their voyage.

crowded, but well-to-do Chinese or merchants also often traveled this way because they could eat the foods they preferred. The Pacific Mail Steamship Company hired Chinese cooks to prepare Chinese meals for its steerage passengers.

At the end of the journey, land was spotted on the horizon, and immigrants prepared to dock at San Francisco Bay or Honolulu Harbor. Joyful that at last they had reached their destination, the immigrants rushed on deck, anxious to watch as their ship sailed into port.

Arrival in the Hawaiian Islands

Immigrants who arrived on the Hawaiian Islands first spotted the lush green mountains rising from the sea. As the ship neared the port, one man was so moved by his landing that he later wrote,

At 8 A.M. we pulled into the immigration station of Honolulu. There was a band playing. We disembarked alphabetically and as we came down the gangplank, they [the immigration officers] asked us where we were going and we shouted the plantation of our destiny. "Waialua Sugar Company!" [or] "Puunene Maui!" people shouted. I shouted, "Haalehu, Hawaii."[15]

Despite their initial thrill at finally arriving, these immigrants soon found that the planters controlled their lives from the moment they landed. After being registered by immigration officers in Honolulu,

The Landing

The reception that immigrants received upon arriving in San Francisco depended largely on when they came. Early immigrants found a friendly greeting from their countrymen already in California. On the other hand, those who arrived toward the end of the nineteenth century faced angry roughnecks.

In his book Strangers from a Different Shore, *Professor Ronald Takaki describes early immigrant Huie Kin's experience when arriving in San Francisco:*

"**O**n a clear, crisp September morning in 1868," after a sixty-day voyage from Guangdong, Huie Kin sighted land. "To be actually at the 'Golden Gate' of the land of our dreams! The feeling that welled up in us was indescribable," he recalled. After Huie and the other passengers had landed "out of the general babble, some one called out in our local dialect [of Cantonese], and, like sheep recognizing the voice only, we blindly followed, and soon were piling into one of the waiting wagons. Everything was so strange and so exciting. . . . The wagon made its way heavily over the cobblestones, turned some corners, ascended a steep climb, and stopped at a clubhouse, where we spent the night."

Later immigrants were not so lucky. According to Takaki, "In China, they [immigrants] had been warned about the 'red-haired, green-eyed' whites with 'hairy faces.' . . . In San Francisco, as they were driven through the streets in wagons, Chinese were often pelted with bricks thrown by white hoodlums. Then, crossing Kearney Street and entering Chinatown, the tired and now bruised travelers were relieved to get away from the *fan qui* ('foreign devils') and glad to find 'Chinese faces delighting the vision, and Chinese voices greeting the ear.'"

the laborers were taken to their assigned plantations. When the men arrived, no matter which island they ended up on, they were housed in huts or barracks on the edge of the cane fields and began work almost immediately.

Arrival in California

Before 1910, Chinese immigrants coming to California were met by relatives or labor contractors at the San Francisco wharf. "As the ship docked, all naturally were excited and tried to put up a good front as they arranged their belongings into tidy bundles," describes author Kil Young Zo. "Most of them wore navy blue cotton clothes and broad rimmed bamboo hats [as they did at home]. All of them had queues [one long braid] which some displayed over their shoulders at full length, while others covered their queues by rolling them over their heads into hats."[16]

Many immigrants left San Francisco immediately in search of gold. From the port, these men began another journey by river from San Francisco Bay to the California goldfields. Those going to northern mines traveled to Sacramento on the Sacramento and American Rivers, while those heading south took the tributaries of the San Joaquin River to the town of Stockton.

The trip to either Stockton or Sacramento lasted only a few days and cost about $16. After buying supplies at the river ports, the miners packed tents, picks, pans, axes, and food and hiked into the foothills of the Sierra Nevada in search of gold.

The Jumping-Off Point

Other immigrants left California entirely following reports of gold discoveries elsewhere in the Western territories. Before long, California became a "jumping-off point" for prospectors heading into Oregon, Washington, Alaska, Utah, Nevada, Colorado, and Idaho. In 1857, the *Oregonian* newspaper read, "the Chinamen are about to take the country [Oregon Territory]. . . . They are buying out the American miners, paying big prices for their claims."[17]

One young miner who trekked to Idaho told his story years later to a newspaper reporter from the *Idaho Daily Statesman*. According to the article,

Chinese men sport traditional Chinese clothing and hairstyles in San Francisco around 1874. San Francisco was the first landing spot for shiploads of Chinese immigrants.

Born in Guangdong Province in 1837, Wong Ying grew up in a poor peasant family. In 1855, he came to the United States on a sailing vessel. . . . Penniless, the young teenager met an "old uncle," [a term Chinese often use for older friends], who gave him $.50 to help start his career in this country. For a while, Wong Ying worked as a cook to save money. The following year, he joined an expedition of Chinese miners headed for the interior of the American West. From Fresno, California, they followed the old Oregon-California Trail all the way to Idaho. Friendly Shoshone and Bannock Indians in Boise Basin furnished the Chinese with meat and showed them placer beds, rich with gleaming gold. At the time, gold was so plentiful that they quickly filled their deerskin bags with heavy nuggets, and at the end of each new moon [every twenty-eight days], they divided the gold among themselves.[18]

By 1863, southern Idaho had become the destination of choice for many Chinese miners. Most Chinese heading for Idaho traveled the overland Chico and Red Bluff Route. Beginning in Sacramento, the trail led prospectors east along the Sacramento River to Chico or Red Bluff and then across the Sierras into the high desert of Nevada and on to Idaho. According to Zhu, this route and the California–Oregon Trail

soon became the main highways carrying the Chinese to the Idaho mining fields. The 600-mile journey required

tremendous endurance and high spirits. . . . Most of the Idaho-bound Chinese, affluent and poor alike, chose to travel on foot. Sometimes a few horses and wagons were used to haul supplies. During the journey, Chinese migrants carried a bamboo stick or wooden pole across their shoulders, and at both ends of the pole, baskets suspended by ropes carried all their personal belongings. Even with fifty or seventy pounds of weight on their shoulders, the Chinese were able to walk quite a distance every day. The entire trip took some two to three months.[19]

This route held all the dangers of traveling on the American frontier. The weather changed from heavy rains to the scorching desert sun to blustery snowstorms on the mountain peaks. Rugged conditions also made many men sick. And like other travelers of the times, the Chinese faced Native American war parties. At least twice during these early years, Indians along the trail killed entire groups of Idaho-bound Chinese.

Immigration Inspection

When California became a state in 1850, all immigrants arriving in San Francisco and elsewhere had to go through immigration inspection. Depending on when and where the immigrants entered the country, they had different experiences. Sung explains,

All Chinese seeking entry to the country . . . used to be detained at the port

Massacre on the Frontier

Some early Chinese immigrants survived the rigors of a difficult ocean crossing only to meet death on their journey to the goldfields. One such group of fifty Chinese immigrants set out from Virginia City, Nevada, to the Boise Basin of Idaho in June 1866. When they neared the Owyhee Crossing on the way to Silver City, a party of about 150 Native American Paiutes ambushed the men. Forty-nine of the prospectors were slain, and only one escaped to tell the story. This is believed to be one of the largest frontier massacres of immigrants in U.S. history.

Following the attack, there was so much anger in Silver City that the community decided to gather a company of men to punish the Paiutes. With Isaac Jennings, a husky miner, as their leader, a group of one hundred men with rations for thirty days set out in search of the war party. The men never found the war party, but when they reached the site of the massacre, they witnessed a terrible scene. They saw the bodies of the immigrants, with their throats cut, strewn along the trail for about two hundred yards. The company dug a twelve-foot-square gravesite and buried the bodies. They never placed a grave marker at the spot, but ten years later a group of travelers passing by reported a garden of wild roses growing at the sunken gravesite along the trail.

of disembarkation [where they got off the boat]. They were taken to Ellis Island [New York], Angel's Island [San Francisco] or some similar detention house [facility]. There they were put under lock and guard until they could be questioned at length. . . . At Ellis Island in New York, at least, the conditions were sanitary and the detainees were not abused. . . .

On the West Coast it was different. . . . For many years, the United States had no immigration building in San Francisco. A shed, rented from the Pacific Mail Steamship Company, served as the detention house. It was a cheap wooden two-story building extending over the water, where the odors of sewage and bilge [water from the ships] gave off a constant stench. . . . Food was served on the floor, and the guards had no qualms about kicking and swearing at the hapless [unfortunate] detainees.[20]

After 1910, Angel Island in San Francisco Bay opened as an inspection facility for officials to interview new immigrants. According to the website of the Angel Island Immigration Station Foundation, "The facility included a barracks, a hospital, utility

Chinese immigrants are interviewed by officials at a crowded San Francisco inspection facility in 1877.

structures, a pier and an administration building. A closer look revealed the locked gates, guard tower, and barbed-wire-topped fences surrounding the station. In its thirty years of operation [1910–1940], it was for many, the 'Gateway to Gold Mountain.'"[21]

When immigrants arrived, they were assigned to men's or women's barracks and given a bunk. Almost immediately afterward, they were examined by health inspectors. Without knowledge of English or Western medical practices, most immigrants were frightened, and the physical examinations seemed "barbaric." Doctors poked sticks down their throats, pulled open their eyelids, and pressed stethoscopes on their bare chests.

Those who were sick returned to China on the next available boat. Immigrants who were deemed healthy by the inspectors had to wait weeks or months, sometimes more than a year, before they spoke with the immigration officers. With a limited number of officers and Chinese interpreters, the process got backed up as more immigrants kept arriving.

Daily life in detention was difficult. While awaiting their interrogation, no one was allowed to depart or to have any visitors. The bare facilities allowed almost no privacy. As one immigrant explained, "'When we arrived they locked us up like criminals in compartments like the cages in the zoo. They counted us and then took us up upstairs to our rooms.' . . . The men were placed in one large room. There were 190 'small boys up to old men, altogether in the same room.'"[22]

The slumlike conditions, lack of privacy, and long weeks lingering at Angel Island made the immigrants feel frustrated and stressed. Some became depressed; a few adults committed suicide. Others waited in silence and carved poems expressing their feelings on the walls of the detention center. According to author Marlon K. Hom, "Many of the Chinese at the Angel Island Wooden Barracks wrote poems expressing their agony, frustration, anger and despair. They would scribble the lines all over the walls of the barracks where they slept. In the 1930s, two detainees copied these scribbles and brought them to San Francisco."[23]

Paper Sons and Daughters

The long interrogations endured by the immigrants were one way for the government to catch people trying to immigrate illegally. Between 1882 and 1943, the U.S. government passed a series of laws aimed at keeping Chinese immigration to a minimum. The Chinese, though, found ways around the laws. For instance, children of an American citizen, even those who had a Chinese mother, were entitled to U.S. citizenship and could not be excluded from

Inspectors search Chinese immigrants for opium in 1882, the first year during which the U.S. government passed laws designed to limit Chinese immigration.

America. Thus, the Chinese devised a system of bringing young people to the country illegally by claiming they were the sons or daughters of immigrants who had American citizenship. Called "paper" sons and daughters, thousands of people immigrated into the United States this way between 1906 and 1943.

In order to entrap paper sons and daughters, there was harsh questioning of all Chinese entering the United States. After waiting long months at Angel Island, immigrants faced a Chinese interpreter and an often unfriendly inspector who asked hundreds of questions: Whose house was first in the third row of your village? Where did you hide the family rice? How many pigs did your family own? When was your sister born? Your mother? Such demands could go on for days as inspectors tried to catch the immigrants in a mistake. Paper sons and daughters who hoped to enter the country had memorized "crib sheets," or coaching books, with pages of numerous facts and specifics about their fictitious lives in China. Still, they could be caught without a correct answer.

A local Chinese minister who worked for many years as an interpreter at Angel Island remembered two boys he helped interview. The inspectors questioned the boys separately and asked (among other things) if the family had owned a dog. The first boy replied, "Yes." Later they asked the second young man the same question. He replied, "No, no dog." The inspectors then recalled the first brother and asked him about the dog and confronted him with his brother's answer. The boy recovered quickly. "Yes," he said, "well, we had a dog, but we knew we were coming to the United States, so we ate the dog."[24]

The two paper brothers were eventually allowed to enter the United States, but those who failed their tests, whether real or paper relatives, were deported back to China. Those who passed were ferried at last to San Francisco, where they began their new lives in America.

CHAPTER THREE

Finding Work in America

Although many Chinese during the mid–nineteenth century came to the United States looking for gold, most were willing to take any employment that offered them the chance to live in America and send some money home. Chinese immigrants found jobs as "house boys" and as paid laborers in agriculture, mining operations, logging camps, and the fishing industry. They formed groups and set out for the mining frontier, where they worked independently as prospectors, cooks, or laundrymen in Western camps. The Chinese immigrants proved so energetic and skillful that many early industries sought them as employees. Their reputa-

tions as hard workers made the builders of the first transcontinental railroad look to the Chinese for the difficult challenge of laying track in the giant mountains of California's Sierra Nevada. And although most remained in the West, a few also traveled to the southern and eastern states in search of jobs.

In the South and the East

After the Civil War in 1865, southern plantation owners looked for labor to replace the newly freed slaves. They believed that the South's economic recovery depended on cheap, productive workers, and many

A Chinese man sets out for work in the California gold mines.

plantation owners in Mississippi and Louisiana hired Chinese immigrants, hoping to have them serve as model workers for ex-slaves. Although most Southerners had never seen Chinese labor, reports from the West told of their willingness to work hard for low wages. A Mississippi newspaper reported, "Messrs. Ferris and Estell, who are cultivating the Hughs place, near Prentiss, recently imported direct from Hong Kong, a lot of Chinese, sixteen in number, with whom as laborers, they are well pleased."[25]

Most of the Chinese workers, though, soon tired of plantation life, where they had poor pay and little freedom, so they went to the cities to find work. There they set up small businesses such as laundries, groceries, and stores. During the 1860s, Chinese laborers also went to the East Coast to work.

They began in the shoe manufacturing industry. New England businessman Calvin T. Sampson recruited Chinese immigrants for his Model Shoe Factory after white workers went on strike in 1861. Hoping to keep wages low and make a big profit, Sampson hired the unsuspecting Chinese to replace his striking workers.

When the seventy-five immigrants arrived in North Adams, Massachusetts, they were met by an angry mob of workers who shouted and threw stones at them. The white workers saw the Chinese as strikebreakers who would take away their jobs and livelihood. But the Chinese laborers stayed and worked hard, learning to run the machines with ease. Although the strikers remained angry with the immigrants, the Chinese labored long hours and made steady wages. Local church people befriended the men and taught them English. After a few years, other manufacturers hired more Chinese immigrants to work in New England.

In the Goldfields

Most Chinese who arrived during the mid–nineteenth century, though, stayed in the West, and many of these started out as miners. By 1855, two-thirds of the Chinese who immigrated to America dug for gold in the California mines. The miners found land, usually along riverbeds, that had some gold, and hoping to find more, they claimed the sites as their territory. Like other prospectors on the frontier, most Chinese gold miners got their "claims" by marking the boundaries of the land and filling out applications in the county's record office, rather than by outright purchase. Sometimes, though, they did buy the rights to work the land from other miners. Much of the land in California was unsettled territory along the northern rivers, in the foothills, and in the mountains. Miners held on to their claims by renewing them annually.

By the late nineteenth century, silver had also been discovered in the West, and like other prospectors, Chinese followed the discoveries. As mining companies found more efficient ways to mine gold, and eventually silver, however, most Chinese gave up their independence and went to work for mining operations already established by U.S. citizens.

During the gold rush days of the 1850s, Chinese immigrants mined for gold along the rivers, streams, and creeks of California and other Western states. They panned by hand or shoveled sand into placers or cradle boxes, which sifted out the dirt and left the heavier gold at the bottom. When Chinese prospectors found gold, they usually remained quiet, fearful that Americans might take away their claim. Many rough

Chinese immigrants pan for gold using placers and cradles during the gold rush of the 1850s.

American miners did resent the immigrants coming to the United States in search of riches. At times, these American miners pushed the Chinese off claims, declaring that foreigners had no right to be in the country.

In May 1852, in response to such widespread feelings, the California legislature passed a law stating that all foreign miners who did not wish to become citizens had to pay a monthly tax of $3. Since the Naturalization Law of 1790 restricted naturalized citizenship to "whites" only, the Chinese were ineligible for citizenship and had no choice but to pay the monthly tax. The Foreign Min-

ers Tax remained in effect until 1870 when it was overruled by the Civil Rights Act, but by then the state had received more than $5 million in taxes from Chinese miners.

Laundrymen

In addition to looking for gold, during the mid–nineteenth century, many immigrants started their own small businesses. Most men in mining and logging towns and camps needed someone to do the cooking and the washing. A man with little strength, money, and scant knowledge of English could start a laundry business for about $5. Such busi-

Chinese Frontier Woman: The Legend of Polly Bemis

Although most Chinese immigrants on the frontier were men, a few women lived and worked there as well. One was Polly Bemis, the most well-known Chinese woman in Idaho history. Bemis was born Lalu Nathoy in 1853 to a poor peasant family in northern China. She spent her early childhood in poverty. Then, according to Polly, when she reached eighteen years of age, her father sold her to bandits for two bags of seeds that her family needed.

The bandits took Polly to the United States and on to mining country. There, the men sold her for $2,500 to Hong King, a saloonkeeper in Warren, Idaho. Polly worked in the saloon a few years until her freedom was won in a poker game by a local miner named Charlie

Bemis. Even after Charlie won her freedom, Polly stayed in Warren, where she used her knowledge of Chinese herbs to nurse local children in times of sickness.

In 1894, Polly married Charlie Bemis, and the couple bought a farm on Idaho's Salmon River. Polly raised chickens, ducks, and cows and fished the river. She planted all kinds of fruit trees—cherry, plum, and pear—and she grew watermelons, strawberries, and blackberries as well as corn and garden vegetables and her healing Chinese herbs.

Polly survived the harsh frontier conditions with her energy and resourcefulness. She was beloved by her neighbors, though, because of her caring and generous spirit.

nesses were popular, and many immigrants found themselves scrubbing clothes on their washboards, hanging them on lines to dry, and ironing shirts on benches with flatirons they heated on the fire. Although they had never done this in China, they learned their trade from American women.

Laundrymen set up their business on a creek or stream where they had plenty of water, and where they could build a shack-like washhouse and live at the site. Miners brought in their clothes to be washed and returned a few days later to pick up their clean laundry.

One laundryman named Lee Chew described such a life on the frontier:

> When I first opened a laundry, it was in company with a partner, who had been in the business for some years. . . . We had to put up with many insults and some frauds, as men would come in and claim parcels that did not belong to them saying they had lost their tickets and would fight if they did not get what they asked for. . . .
>
> We were [there for] three years . . . [and] we made plenty of money in gold dust, but had a hard time, for many of the miners were wild men who carried revolvers and after drinking would come into our place to shoot and steal shirts.[26]

Agriculture and the Fishing Industry

Chinese workers also made major contributions in agriculture and the fishing in-

Some industrious Chinese immigrants started their own laundry businesses on the frontier.

dustry. Most of the immigrants had been farmers at home, so when they arrived in America, some of them turned to farming to earn a living. The valleys in the West contained rich soils. Some Chinese began by providing food for those in the mining camps, and they often found they could make more money by farming their claims than by digging for gold or silver.

Many also became "truck gardeners," raising vegetables and fruits and delivering their products by foot or wagon to towns to sell. Some truck gardeners eventually purchased their land, but most leased or sharecropped it (meaning they gave a percentage of their crop to the landowners as payment for using the land). Laboring long hours, the Chinese were quick to learn new skills

Chinese workers labor at a Louisiana sugar plantation in 1871. Chinese immigrants proved that they were hard workers and could learn new skills quickly.

and grow more crops. They soon dominated the strawberry and sugar beet industries of California.

During the mid–nineteenth century, truck farmers grew a variety of crops for market. According to historian Sucheng Chan in *The Bittersweet Soil,*

> Some peddlers traveled great distances, making round trips that measured hundreds of miles. For example, an eyewitness remembers a Chinese vegetable-peddler, Tu Charley, a well-known character in the Yuba River basin in the 1890s, who carried fresh cucumbers, tomatoes, beans, melons, and other produce in a horse-drawn wagon, traveling periodically between Marysville and Sierra City [California], a distance of over a hundred miles in hilly terrain. Both the short-distance vegetable-peddler, who carried his produce in baskets suspended on a bamboo pole balanced across his shoulder, and the long-distance vegetable-peddler, who used a horse-drawn cart or pack mules, were adapting an ancient Chinese practice to the California environment.[27]

Other immigrants labored for large landowners rather than for themselves. Bringing thousands of new acres under cultivation, they drained swamplands, built levees, and dug irrigation canals. As farmhands they plowed, planted, pruned, and harvested the yield for others. Two immigrants even developed new varieties of fruit. Ah Bing, a Chinese horticulturist in Oregon, grew the sweet-tasting Bing cherry, and Lue Gin Gone grafted the frost-resistant Lue orange. Up and down the West Coast as migrant labor, the Chinese picked hops (a plant used in medicines and beer), dug potatoes, and harvested wheat.

In orchards, they plucked apples, peaches, plums, and pears. After the crops were in, they packed and canned the fruits and vegetables for market. Their labor helped make California one of the richest agriculture states in the country.

During the mid–nineteenth century, too, many peasants took up fishing and built a fishing industry on the West Coast. Using

A Fishing Industry in San Diego Bay

One of the earliest fishing industries on the West Coast was started by Chinese fishermen who emigrated from the Pearl River Delta in Guangdong province. By 1869, two fishing villages sat on the shores of San Diego, California. The first settlement was along the bay at Point Loma. There, the immigrants put up their shanties and drying racks and built their sailing junks and sampans. The second village was along the waterfront of what was then called New Town. (Now it is near the harbor where the San Diego Convention Center stands.) Here, the fishermen constructed redwood shacks on stilts, because in those days the area was a tidal mudflat.

The junks built in San Diego all had at least two masts and were made of California redwood (their rudders were made of ironwood from China). The junks proved fast and able to withstand the rough summer storms. Fishermen sailed south to the tip of Baja California, Mexico, and north along the coast to Monterey Bay, gathering all kinds of fish and shellfish, including shrimp, mullet, barracuda, sheepshead, scallops, and the Chinese delicacy, abalone. The San Diego abalone fishermen became the largest exporters on the West Coast, selling more than seven hundred tons a year. Much of their catch, they dried on the beach before shipping to China or to communities in the United States. The fishing industry became a major part of the San Diego economy, and at one time, up to eighteen junks called San Diego Bay home.

After 1882, exclusion laws brought an end to Chinese participation in the fishing industry. The new laws considered foreign waters to begin three miles off the coastline. This meant if Chinese fishermen sailed beyond the three-mile limit of the coast, they had left the United States and would be unable to return to the country. By 1893, only one junk remained. The Chinese fishermen of San Diego found other work or returned to China.

the knowledge of marine life they had acquired in China, they harvested the sea, taking abalone, shrimp, octopus, salmon, and other fish from Mexico to Alaska. They then dried, cleaned, and canned the yield to sell.

Building the Central Pacific Railroad

As the American West grew and landowners sent new crops to the east and industry provided new goods, the long months' journey by wagon to or from the East or the sail around South America proved too lengthy for merchandise or people. To solve the problem, Congress approved plans to build the first transcontinental railroad to connect the East and West Coasts by train. This would reduce the length of the journey from months to days.

The two companies that had raised enough money to undertake the construction were given the contracts. The Central Pacific Railroad Company would start building from the West, and the Union Pacific Railroad Company would begin from the East. The two sets of tracks would meet in the middle. The railroad companies would receive payments from Congress based on the number of miles of track they laid.

The Central Pacific found it difficult to hire enough men to accomplish the gigantic task. The work was hard, as men struggled to lay track through some of the roughest terrain in the country. Many men began but soon quit to find easier work. One of the builders, Charlie Crocker, suggested that the Central Pacific hire Chinese

labor because they had a reputation as good steady workers. Head of operations James Strobridge, however, disagreed at first, saying Chinese men were too short and too light to do the rugged work. "They built the Great Wall of China, didn't they?"[28] replied Crocker.

Finally unable to hire enough men to do the job, Strobridge agreed to try Chinese workers for a month. In 1865, the Central Pacific hired fifty Chinese immigrants to lay the tracks east from Sacramento. After only a few days, Strobridge saw that the immigrants laid the tracks faster than any of the previous crews. Furthermore, they appeared early each morning ready for another full day of work. The Central Pacific then hired as many Chinese as it could, putting them in gangs of twelve to twenty men who worked under a Chinese foreman, called a "China boss."

The China boss gave instructions to his crew and assigned the jobs to be done. One man was chosen to shop, cook meals, and boil tea, while the others chopped down trees, hauled logs, leveled ground, and put down rails. They became hardworking, cheap labor for the railroad; they got paid $10 less per month than white workers.

The first one hundred miles of track went down easily. Then after a few days they reached the Sierra Nevada in eastern California, which rose more than seven thousand feet. Conquering the mountains would require great skill, because the workers had to construct roadbeds on the steep mountainsides. New techniques had to be developed to build along these sheer slopes. Again, railroad officials would call on the Chinese.

A camp for Chinese workers during construction of the first transcontinental railroad. The Chinese workers were an efficient, reliable source of cheap labor for the railroad company.

Putting Ancient Skills to Work

Beginning in the summer of 1865, railroad workers had to make cuts in the rocks, trying to carve a road around the mountainside before they could lay down tracks. First, workers lowered men by ropes down the sides on boson's chairs, swinglike seats used to adjust sail riggings on ships. Dangling in their chairs, the men used black powder to blast away enough space for others to stand. It was a dangerous job, and several men died before they could be hauled back up out of reach of the flying earth and rock.

The Chinese watched and felt they could do a better job, for they knew how to lower men safely down steep slopes in large woven baskets. Moreover, the Chinese had invented gunpowder and had used it for cen-

turies to blast away rock. According to historian Stephen E. Ambrose,

One day in the summer of 1865, a Chinese foreman went to Strobridge, nodded, and waited for permission to speak. When it was granted, he said that men of China were skilled at work like this. Their ancestors had built fortresses in the Yangtze gorges [high mountain walls in China]. Would he permit Chinese crews to work on Cape Horn [the steep mountain]? If so, could reeds be sent up from San Francisco to weave into baskets?

Strobridge [was desperate and] would try anything. The reeds came. At night the Chinese wove baskets similar to the ones their ancestors had used. The baskets were round, waist-high, four eyelets at the top, painted with [good luck] symbols. Ropes ran from the eyelets to a central cable. The Chinese went to work—they needed little or no instruction in handling black powder, which was a Chinese invention—with a hauling crew at the precipice [top].[29]

To carve away the mountainside, each Chinese blaster climbed into a basket, and the crew lowered him over the side of the cliff. Standing in the basket, he bore a hole in the rock with a small hand drill. Next he packed in the black powder and set the fuse. With great care, he lit the fuse and yelled to be pulled up. With the explosion, down came a chunk of the mountain. From their first success, Chinese immigrants took over the blasting jobs, hanging in their baskets as they set the charges and ignited the explosives, slowly cutting away the rock.

The Chinese were called on again when going around the slopes proved difficult. They took on the challenging task of drilling through the granite rock to dig tunnels through the mountain. Working around the clock to make as much progress as possible, men swung pickaxes against the solid wall, breaking down the rock, chip by chip. Others, meanwhile, jammed their shovels into the debris and loaded it into rubble baskets. Still others shouldered the baskets on the ends of long poles and carried out the rocks.

A Dangerous Job

Digging the tunnel was dangerous work, but even more perilous was blasting inside

White men taunt Chinese railroad workers; in the background, a section of mountainside is blasted away.

the tunnel. Men held drills against the rock walls while those with sledgehammers pounded the butt ends. One slip of the heavy hammer and the drill man could be hit on the skull. When there was a big enough hole, someone packed the powder and lit the fuse, and then everyone ran to escape the flying rubble. Occasionally, unexploded powder remained hidden in the granite rock, and unexpected discharges killed men when their drilling hammers hit and ignited the charge. Despite the dangers and accidents, this blasting method seemed too slow for boss James Strobridge. With even more risk, he called for doubling up on the powder and finally decided to use volatile nitroglycerin.

Nitroglycerin was so explosive that the ingredients to make it were hauled up to the mountain before being mixed together. (The two ingredients could not detonate until blended together.) None of the workers except the Chinese were willing to use it. The nitroglycerin proved more powerful than the black gunpowder in blowing away the rock, but there were also more accidents and more men killed.

Although blasting with nitroglycerin was extremely dangerous, and several men died, the Chinese kept on the job until they got through the tunnel. Lewis Clement, an engineer for the railroad, wrote a report saying, "the rock was so hard that it seemed impossible to drill into it a sufficient depth for blasting purposes. . . . Perseverance alone conquered [the mountain]."[30] Despite the hazards, Strobridge pushed the Chinese laborers to work faster and faster to keep on schedule, and the men toiled around the clock.

Time was essential in receiving money from Congress, but tunneling through the mountains went slowly despite working day and night shifts. By the winter of 1866, the Central Pacific required its men to work despite frigid winds and blowing snow. Sometimes snow drifted forty to sixty feet high, covering construction sites. At other times, avalanches buried men and camps, and some bodies were not found until the snows melted in the spring.

On December 28, 1866, as the men labored to blast a passage through the tunnel, the *Sacramento Union* newspaper described the situation:

The portals of the summit tunnel were buried under fantastic [snow] drifts, and the Chinese encampments were snowed under. The Chinese dug chimneys and air shafts, [and] lived by lantern light. They tunneled in from the camps to reach the bore of the tunnel itself, and the work continued, although materials now had to be lowered forty feet or more by steam hoist from the surface of the [deep] snow, and the waste from the digging taken out in the same way.[31]

By 1869, the Central Pacific Railroad had hired about ten thousand Chinese to lay track, carve tunnels, and blast through the mighty Sierra. For their efforts, each man was paid $30 to $36 a month, while whites received $40 to $46. In response to the lower pay and longer workdays, the Chinese went on strike. About half the Chinese workers refused to leave their camp until they received the same treatment as white laborers. In response, Charlie Crocker cut off the strikers' food and water, and after a week the men were too hungry and thirsty to continue. They returned to work.

A Chinese Accomplishment

Regardless of the difficulties, the Chinese proved indomitable as they conquered the Sierra Nevada and laid the tracks through some of the most rugged lands and in the worst weather in the country. Hundreds of Chinese laborers perished from accidents, cruel winter storms, the burning sun of the high desert, or the diseases that spread among men living in such harsh conditions.

The construction of the Central Pacific Railroad was truly a Chinese accomplishment. Without their skills and hard work,

Workers celebrate the joining of the Central Pacific and Union Pacific railroad lines at Promontory Point, Utah, on May 10, 1869.

the railroad could never have been completed when it was. The builders worked six days a week from sunrise to sunset. Whatever the season, the landscape, the weather, or the job to be done, they pushed on through California to Nevada and Utah to meet the Union Pacific at Promontory Point, Utah, on May 10, 1869. The Chinese laborers' hard work and persistence earned them high praise from Strobridge, who said, "They learn quickly, do not fight, have no strikes that amount to anything, and are very cleanly in their habits. They will gamble and do quarrel among themselves most noisily—but harmlessly."[32]

A celebration marked the joining of the tracks of the Central Pacific Railroad with the Union Pacific Railroad. Two men from the Central Pacific and two from the Union Pacific came forward to lay the last tie. A group of Chinese immigrants, dressed up in clean blue shirts and pants, carried the Western rail, and an Irish immigrant squad hauled the one from the East. Railroad officials placed the final tie on the ground, and a golden spike was driven into the track to mark the achievement.

Soon afterward, the Central Pacific Railroad discharged most of its Chinese laborers, although a few did stay on to keep tracks open or to build new branch lines in the Southwest. Some of the unemployed heard about new discoveries of gold in southern Idaho; they packed up and trekked more than a hundred miles to get there. Others went to work in agriculture or the expanding Western industries. A few returned to China.

CHAPTER FOUR

Forming Communities in the West

The earliest Chinese immigrants to the United States came as single men planning to return to China. After a few years, though, many found they wanted to settle in the new country. Thus, by the turn of the twentieth century, a few had brought their wives and children to live with them, and immigrants had begun to set up communities where they could live, work, and educate their children.

These communities, called Chinatowns, evolved from Chinese sections of frontier settlements into lively city districts. As more immigrants arrived, the small sections became more and more crowded. Lodging houses crowded men in tiny rooms. Whole families slept all in one room or used part of their living space for work, clearing away bedding in the morning and using tables for folding laundry or cutting cloth during the day. And shopkeepers remained busy from morning till night, as immigrants did most of their business in the Chinese district.

Chinese Exclusion Acts

The populations in these Chinatowns grew year after year until the U.S. government's passage of the exclusion acts. In 1882, President Chester Arthur, in response to growing American prejudice, signed the Chinese

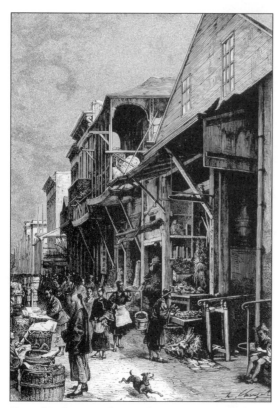

People shop and mingle on a crowded street in San Francisco's Chinatown, around 1878.

Exclusion Act, which said that for ten years only a small number of Chinese immigrants could enter the United States. Those with a special purpose for coming, such as teachers, students, travelers, and merchants, could still come, and those already living in the country could remain. All others, however, were no longer welcome. The legislation also denied citizenship to Chinese immigrants living in the United States and went on to add that any laws saying otherwise were no longer valid. After the implementation of the Exclusion Act, almost all Chinese immigration to America came to a halt; in 1885, just twenty-two Chinese immigrated to the United States. The exclu-

sion law was renewed in 1892 and extended indefinitely in 1902.

Other laws supported these exclusions. In 1888, the Scott Act prohibited Chinese laborers from immigrating. This meant Chinese who wanted to return home for a visit had to obtain a "reentry permit" to be allowed back into the United States. Thus, many people who had gone to China for short trips to see relatives but could not get a reentry permit were forbidden from returning to America. As a result, about thirty thousand sojourners visiting China were denied reentry even though they had jobs or families awaiting their return.

A loophole in the exclusion laws, though, made it possible for families of merchants and families of citizens to enter the country. Many of the Chinese workers who lived in the United States were anxious to bring over their wives and children; thus, they often claimed to be merchants. In addition, after immigration records were destroyed in the San Francisco earthquake of 1906, thousands of Chinese men claimed citizenship and brought their wives and children to America. Between 1907 and 1924, about ten thousand Chinese women came to the United States.

Xenophobia

Even before the exclusion acts, individual Western states had passed laws against the Chinese, and state courts had often accepted the laws as constitutional. The California Supreme Court, for instance, declared in 1854 that no Chinese immigrant could testify in court against a "white person." This meant that crimes like theft and destruction of property perpetrated by whites against Chinese went unpunished, since the immigrants were unable to testify in their own defense.

Supported by laws like these, xenophobia, or hatred of foreigners, became commonplace across the United States. Chinese immigrants were frequently attacked, and authorities often took no action against whites who robbed or even murdered Chinese. One newspaper declared on December 18, 1856,

> Hundreds of Chinamen have been slaughtered in cold blood during the last five years by desperadoes that infest our state [California]. The murder of Chinamen was almost a daily occurrence, yet in all this time we have heard of but two or three instances where the guilty parties have been brought to justice and punished according to law.[33]

Although there were people who recognized the contributions the Chinese had made to the railroad, agriculture, and other industries, they were not a majority, and violence and racial prejudice erupted in the West. As author Betty Lee Sung writes,

> In 1878, the entire Chinese population of Truckee [California] was rounded up and driven from town.

> In 1885, the infamous massacre of 28 Chinese in Rock Springs, Wyoming, occurred. Many others were wounded and hundreds were driven from their homes [by white coal miners].

In 1885, a mob of white coal miners, angry with the Chinese for working during a miners' strike, massacred twenty-eight Chinese immigrants in Rock Springs, Wyoming.

In 1886, Long Cabin, Oregon, was the scene of another brutal massacre. . . .

Murdering Chinese became such a common place occurrence that the newspapers seldom bothered to print the stories. Police officials winked at the attacks, and politicians all but incited more of the same.[34]

Unwilling to Live Among the Chinese

Throughout the 1870s, many Chinese moved from pioneer communities to cities, fleeing such attacks. And by the 1900s, as the frontier life faded, prejudice against them had become less violent and more hidden. Many whites harbored resentment and disliked the idea of Chinese immigrants living among them. When Chinese families tried to integrate into the broader society, they found it difficult.

An editor of a Chinese daily newspaper in Los Angeles, who spoke excellent English (as did his wife and children), provides an example. He and his wife dressed in Western styles, were members of a Presbyterian church, and followed American traditions; still, they faced prejudice. He explained,

In the summer of 1901 I proposed to bring my family from Los Angeles to San Francisco. I tried many times to find a suitable house outside of Chinatown so that my children might be properly brought up in the ways of the Americans, that in the years to come they may perform the duties of American citizenship.

I found a good flat with five rooms and bath and the rent was within my ability to pay. The landlady was willing also to rent the house to me after having heard the explanation I made regarding myself. The rent was paid and preparation was made for moving in, but after two days the landlady came to my office and returned the money to me and explained the situation: the whole neighborhood had risen in arms against the idea of having a Chinese family in their midst. . . .

A few weeks later I again tried my luck, and in the course of the afternoon, I found two houses. . . . The agents kindly made arrangements to rent the premises to me but when the landlords were apprised of the nationality of their prospective tenants all arrangements were annulled.

After all these failures, I was not yet dismayed, I resolved to try again. . . . I found a flat on Mason Street near Sacramento. . . . So he [the landlord] agreed to rent the place . . . , [but two days later] he told me it was out of the question to rent to me since the other tenants objected strenuously. . . . From that time on I never made another move. The proverbial Chinese perseverance seemed to have left me for good.[35]

Because they were not welcomed in most neighborhoods, the Chinese had little choice but to live separate lives. In her article on the Chinese in *The Reference Li-*

The influence of Chinese architecture, including curved, tile roofs and Chinese-language signs, is evident in this modern photograph of San Francisco's Chinatown.

brary of Asian Americans, Connie Young Yu notes, "By the 1920s, Chinese were barred [by state laws] from owning land, from performing certain occupations, and from entering all but the fringes of U.S. society. They were perpetual aliens [foreigners]. . . . Suspicious of government and far from the mainstream, they were regarded as stubbornly clannish outsiders.[36]

Living in Chinatowns

For this reason, most Chinese families congregated in Chinatowns. During the 1840s and 1850s, immigrants arriving in San Francisco, for instance, bought or rented land

near a place then known as Portsmouth Plaza (now called Portsmouth Square). As more immigrants arrived, they expanded north and south along Calle de Fundacion (later Dupont Street and today called Grant Avenue). By the 1880s, San Francisco's Chinese had filled their region of the city with small restaurants, general stores, Chinese herbal shops, apothecaries, boardinghouses, and meat markets. Stores carried goods imported from China such as teas, dried herbs, dried fish, dried ducks, fans, shawls, and even pots and pans. Street peddlers carried fresh Chinese vegetables and fruits in their baskets. During the day and often into the evenings, the streets bustled with business

SOME OF THE LARGER CHINATOWNS IN THE UNITED STATES

Seattle

Sacramento
San Francisco

Los Angeles

Honolulu

Chicago

Houston

Boston
New York
Philadelphia
Washington, DC

and companionship as men gathered to talk on street corners and share news.

As in San Francisco, Chinatowns sprang up all over the West in cities like Los Angeles, Sacramento, and Marysville, California, and in the East in Boston and New York. In these locations, immigrants set up their own societies as closely resembling their homeland as possible. Chinatowns included Buddhist or Taoist temples, opera houses, social clubs, banks, hospitals, and schools, and in many places by the twentieth century the owners had remodeled the buildings to resemble those of China, complete with curved and tiled roofs, pagodas (temples), lanterns, courtyards, and gardens. Dragons (a powerful Chinese symbol) curled around columns supporting roofs, and lion figures (a ferocious sign to the Chinese) crouched on their haunches, guarding entrances.

As Chinatowns in the West added Chinese pagodas and square buildings with upturned tile-roof corners, Eastern Chinatowns like that in New York City used distinct colors and signs with Chinese characters to remind the inhabitants of home. Describing New York's Chinatown, journalist and reformer Jacob A. Riis wrote in 1890,

Mott Street [where the Chinese had settled] is clean to distraction. The laundry stamp is on it, though the houses are chiefly of the conventional tenement-house type, with nothing to rescue them from the everyday dismal dreariness of their kind save here and there a splash of dull red or yellow, a sign, hung endways and with streamers of red flannel tacked on, that announces in Chinese characters that Dr. Chay Yen Chong sells Chinese herb medicines, or that Won Lung & Co . . . take in washing, or deal out tea and groceries.[37]

Going into Business

As the years passed, the Chinatowns prospered. Although nineteenth-century merchants set up shops there to serve the Chinese community, by the twentieth century some businesses like laundries, restaurants, variety stores, and groceries served the needs of the broader community. Tourists and locals alike were drawn to the unique culture in their cities' Chinese sections. However, even though outsiders came into Chinatown, those Chinese who wanted to move outside the district still faced prejudice.

Laundries, Restaurants, and Groceries

Within the Chinatowns, families tended to start businesses that offered some kind of service. The Chinese set up laundries as permanent businesses, and whole families worked to make a living. The laundries typically included a front section for ironing and waiting on customers. Behind this was the room where the family slept; because quarters were cramped, this room often also contained storage space for the laundry. Sometimes a drying room was at the rear, with lines strung up to hold wet clothes.

Chinese families also opened restaurants. Although Chinese men had not cooked in China, in Chinatowns during the mid–nineteenth century, many men made their living cooking for others. Chinese characters announced restaurants with names like "Fragrant Tea Chamber," "Chamber of Odors of Distant Lands," or "Fragrant Almond Chamber." By the 1890s, Chinese restaurants had spread across the country as Americans discovered the delicious tastes of traditional Chinese cooking. After 1906, when many wives had immigrated to the United States, many husband and wife teams ran the restaurants. Often a husband cooked and washed dishes, while the wife worked as a waitress, barmaid, and cashier.

Chinese grocery and merchandise stores also began with the earliest arrivals, but as time went on these varied in size. Some stores were large, dividing up the work—bookkeeping, cleaning, waiting on

A woman purchases meat at a Chinese butcher shop in San Francisco in the 1950s.

customers, cooking, and whatever else needed to be done—among several partners. After the San Francisco earthquake, though, many immigrant families opened smaller stores. In these shops, family members provided the labor, working long hours shelving, packing, keeping the accounts, and selling goods without any salary.

One example is Chin Shee, who came to San Francisco and worked with her merchant husband at the family dry goods store. She, her husband, and their six children lived in the rear of the store. Her great-granddaughter wrote, "She not only took care of her children, but also helped with her husband's business. All the hard work and responsibilities made her face appear 'careworn' in middle age."[38]

Tongs, *Fongs*, and District Associations

Family businesses were the norm in Chinatowns because maintaining close ties was important to the Chinese way of life. Another way the immigrants maintained these ties, and made the unfamiliar United States seem less strange, was by starting traditional community organizations. These organizations—tongs, *fongs*, and district associations—whose ideals traveled with the immigrants across the Pacific, fostered a sense of community and belonging in a sometimes hostile new country.

In Guangdong province, organizations known as *tongs* were first organized as secret movements against the Manchu government. Because so many *tong* members immigrated to the United States, these

The Chinese-Language Newspapers

Since immigrants tended to live in communities with their own people and tended to speak their own tongue, it was common to have newspapers printed in their native language. The Chinese were no exception, printing several newspapers in the United States in their own language. The first, the *Golden Hills News,* began in 1854 in San Francisco. Others followed soon after: also in San Francisco, the *Oriental* and *Chinese Free Press;* in Sacramento, the *Chinese Daily News;* in Honolulu, the *New China Daily News;*

and in New York, the *Chinese Reform News.* Many of the Chinese immigrants were illiterate, however, and following the institution of the exclusion laws, their population decreased. As a result, most of the newspapers folded.

The *Chinese World,* published in both English and Chinese in San Francisco beginning in 1891 was one that survived. It held considerable influence on the Chinese American community and was a voice for those wanting reform in China. This paper continued to publish until 1969.

groups found their way into American Chinatowns, and in doing so, their purpose changed. In the new country, the tongs provided friendship and help to recently arrived immigrants. In 1852, the first tong, *Kwang-tek-ton* (Chamber of Far-Reaching Virtue), was established in California. It offered companionship as well as protection from whites or opposing tong members. Because tongs met the needs of the immigrants, they became common in America, moving eastward across the country as the immigrants moved. "We are strangers in a strange country," one tong member said. "We must have an organization [tong] to control our country fellows and develop friendship."[39]

The immigrants also formed *fongs,* groups of family and village members. In America, various *fongs* set up clubhouses, which served as residences and gathering places. Together, *fong* members established temples and networks to send letters back home. They also held funerals and buried deceased community members or shipped the remains to China to be buried with ancestors.

Finally, the immigrants established *huiguan,* "district associations," whose membership depended on the area or region in China from which the immigrants had originally come. The district associations supported the community by meeting the immigrants at the port and finding them housing and jobs. Between 1851 and 1862, six major *huiguan,* representing various regions in China, were organized in California. These were the Sze Yup Association, the Ning Yeung Association, the Sam Yup Association, the Yeong Wo Association, the Hop Wo Association, and the Yan Wo Association. To give the Chinese a strong organization to represent their needs to the mainstream American community, the six associations joined together in the 1860s and became known as the Chinese Six Companies.

The Chinese Six Companies

Besides acting as an organization to improve the position of the Chinese in the United States, the Chinese Six Companies acted as a local government for immigrants in Chinese communities across the country. A chairman was elected from the association members to head the organization. There was also a council of fifty-five seats, chosen from each district to represent its members. The Chinese Six Companies settled disputes within Chinatown and provided health and educational services. They also operated as the representative of the Chinese community to the city officials and state governments and hired white lawyers to fight unjust laws against the Chinese.

Most of the leaders of the Chinese Six Companies were successful merchants who had dealings with white businessmen in San Francisco and other cities. Because of their contacts, these Chinese leaders could go to public officials or influential Americans with the Chinese community's problems. Often, these officials proved sympathetic to the Chinese situation. As a result, the Chinese Six Companies were able to get white men to speak for them in courts and meetings where the Chinese themselves were excluded. In this manner, the Chinese Six

Chinese Six Companies Battle Discrimination

The Chinese Six Companies had been organized to help the immigrants with their life in a strange new land. It soon became clear that one of the best ways to help the Chinese was to fight discriminatory laws passed against them. And the best chance to strike down unfair laws, the Chinese Six Companies felt, was in the courts.

The Chinese Six Companies hired white lawyers to work against laws that singled out the Chinese. Their lawyers found some success over the years in overturning some of the most biased legislation. For example, in 1879 in the case of *Ho Ah Kow v. Sheriff Matthew Nunam,* Judge Steven Field ruled that the queue ordinance, which required men held in jail to have short hair, violated the Civil Rights Act of 1870, the Fourteenth Amendment, and provisions of the Burlingame Treaty between the United States and China. Another such victory came in 1885 when the California Supreme Court ruled it was unconstitutional to forbid Chinese children access to public schools.

Companies were often able to get laws and regulations against the Chinese changed.

Education in Chinatown

Despite the assistance of the Chinese Six Companies, the Chinese living in the United States still faced problems both in and out of their section of town. Americans tended to shun the immigrants and their families. Sometimes, things even turned violent. Recalling San Francisco's Chinatown during the 1870s, Huie Kin said, "We were simply terrified; we kept indoors after dark for fear of being shot in the back. [If we wandered outside Chinatown,] children spit upon us as we passed by and called us rats."[40]

Because of such strong prejudice, especially in California, gaining an education proved to be a challenge. In 1859, the superintendent of public instruction in California declared that children of Chinese, Negroes, and American Indians should not be allowed to attend school with white children, although separate schools could be established for them. At that time, there were only about five hundred Chinese children of school age in the state. Some of those were admitted into country schools with white students. Others, though, primarily Chinese students in cities, had to attend either private or church schools for their education.

In San Francisco in 1884, the superintendent's ruling was tested. Eight-year-old Mamie Tape tried to enter a city school. Mamie had been born in the United States, but school officials refused to let her enroll in that or any other city school. Frustrated, her parents decided to take legal action and contacted a lawyer who took the case to court. In 1885, the California Supreme Court agreed with the Tapes, saying, "To deny a child, born of Chinese parents in this State, entrance to the public schools would be a violation of the law of the State and the Constitution of the United States."[41] Thus, forced to enroll Mamie, the San Francisco school board established the first segregated Chinese primary school in Chinatown. The board rented space over a grocery store and hired American teachers. Mamie and her younger brother Frank became the school's first students.

For most Chinese immigrant children, public schools were where they initially learned American traditions. Jade Snow Wong remembers her experience at a public school in San Francisco's Chinatown:

The schoolteacher . . . spoke in the foreign English language. . . . [And] she discouraged them [her pupils] from speaking their accustomed [Chinese] language. . . .

New games in the foreign language were learned—Farmer in the Dell, Go Walking Around the Valley, London Bridge Is Falling Down. . . . [I] memorized a poem about Jack and Jill who climbed up a hill to get water but somehow lost it all.

Chinese immigrants often faced discrimination and prejudice, even violence. This illustration depicts an anti-Chinese riot that occurred in Seattle, Washington, in 1886.

Instead of opening on the left-hand side and reading from right to left in vertical rolls like Chinese books, the new books with gay, colored pictures opened on the right-hand side and were read horizontally from left to right.[42]

Religious Schools

Eventually, all students of Chinese heritage were allowed to attend public schools, but many of these also simultaneously attended special Chinese evening schools, usually sponsored by a church. In these schools, the children learned to read and write Chinese; their parents hoped they would be literate in the language of their ancestors. Jade Snow Wong says,

Immigrant children learn the English language at a Chinese school in New York.

she walked a few blocks from her home to attend the Hip Wo Chinese evening school, which was operated and subsidized jointly by the American boards and Chinese branches of three churches: Presbyterian, Congregational, and Methodist. The worst part of the Chinese school was that it left [me] without any time to play with Jade Precious Stone [my younger sister] after school, or chat with Grandmother or to observe the daily changing antics of [my baby] brother [named] Forgiveness. After school there was scarcely an hour left for folding diapers and getting something to eat before starting to the Chinese school. School was not dismissed until 8:00 P.M., after which there were lessons at home.[43]

For Chinese adults wanting to learn English, churches across the country also established religious Sunday schools. Organizers of these schools hoped to teach the immigrants English so they could read the scriptures, convert to Christianity, and perhaps return to China as missionaries. Teachers in these schools taught both English and religion, and many also helped the adult immigrants learn more about American life and customs.

As Chinese communities grew, they created schools, organizations, structures, associations, and businesses aimed at making America feel more accessible and familiar. Chinatowns often remained poor sections of cities, but within their boundaries, residents lived and worked among people who spoke their language and understood their culture, a situation that proved to be welcomed and valued by the Chinese community.

CHAPTER FIVE

Working and Forming Communities in Hawaii

California was not the only place to which Chinese immigrants traveled. Many Chinese from Guangdong also chose to immigrate to Hawaii. Like those who sailed to the American West, they went to earn money to send home. Once they arrived, though, their experiences differed markedly from those of the immigrants who went to the mainland. From the beginning, Hawaiians were more accepting of cultural and ethnic differences, and the Chinese soon blended in to Hawaiian society. As scholar Clarence E. Glick says, "there were more educational, economic, and social opportunities for Hawaiian-born Chinese in the Islands' multiethnic community."[44]

The Chinese also made efforts to adjust to life in Hawaii. The Chinese and Hawaiians intermarried, blending families and helping assimilation. And from the beginning, many immigrants learned to speak Hawaiian. Reverend William Spear wrote to a friend in 1856 that one of the most amusing sights he had found in Hawaii was two men from China, who spoke different Cantonese dialects, using the Hawaiian language to talk to each other.

Life on Plantations

Almost all Chinese who immigrated to Hawaii after 1850 were poor peasants who

Chinese plantation workers in Hawaii lived in communal barracks like these and worked six days a week.

left China under the "labor contract" system. Under this system, each man signed a contract to work for three to five years. In exchange, the plantation owner paid the man's passage to Hawaii and agreed to pay him a wage of a few dollars a month. Peasants also often received a wage advance in order to buy things they needed for the journey—a jacket, change of clothes, or bedding. Then, once the immigrants arrived in Hawaii, the planters provided them with a place to live, food, and medical care.

Although the Chinese going to Hawaii freely signed job contracts before they left China, once they arrived, they had little control over their daily lives. The men lived with six to forty others in simple but clean huts or barracks on the plantation grounds. A whistle blew to call the men to work at dawn every day except Sunday, and a luna (foreman) grouped the laborers into gangs

of twenty to thirty to work in the cane fields. They traveled to the cane fields or sugar mill on foot or in horse-drawn wagons. In the fields, they planted and cut the cane. Once it was ready, the men helped haul it to the mill, where it was made into sugar. As Tin-Yuke Char explains in his book *The Sandalwood Mountains,*

[The work] comprises clearing land, cutting wood and brush, grubbing out roots, moving rocks and brush . . . , hoeing, irrigating, fertilizing, planting, stripping and cutting cane, loading or unloading cane cars, and any other necessary farming operations. In and about the mill they are occupied in feeding the cane carrier and furnaces, tending any of the mill machinery, handling sugar, loading [railroad] cars.[45]

During the 1880s, other immigrant groups came to Hawaii, including Japanese, Korean, Filipino, Portuguese, and Spanish, and planters built new camps and segregated their labor by ethnic groups. Resentment sometimes arose among the various groups because some plantations encouraged competition between them. But other plantations were integrated from the beginning, and people of differing backgrounds lived side by side. By the early twentieth century, most plantation workers had learned to live and work together. In doing so, they forged strong friendships and were able to negotiate better working conditions for all plantation labor.

Hawaii Wants Women

For the first thirty years, most of the Chinese immigrants to Hawaii were men who lived in bachelor communities on the plantation grounds. When their contracts were up, these men often left the plantations to start small businesses and families in local villages. In an effort to keep the men working on the plantations, planters encouraged the migration of Chinese women and families.

Hawaiian newspaper editorials praised women's influence as homemakers and wrote of their importance in developing a wholesome society. Christian ministers agreed, and in 1881 missionary Frank Damon wrote,

No surer safeguard can be erected against the thousand possible ills which may arise from the indiscriminate herding together of thousands of men! Let the sweet and gentle influence of the mother, the wife, the sister and the daughter be brought to bear upon the large yearly increasing company of Chinese in our midst, and we shall soon see a change wrought, such as police regulations cannot produce.[46]

At first, the women worked alongside the men on the plantations. Some labored in the fields weeding and hoeing; others remained in camp to cook, wash, and sew. As they spent more time in Hawaii and as families moved off the plantations, many Chinese women found work outside the home. And by the early twentieth century, many young Chinese women had gained a college education and found employment in the American workforce, including the teaching profession.

Many women worked alongside men in the Hawaiian sugar fields.

Integrated Families

Many Chinese men also married Hawaiian women. By 1900, about fifteen hundred Chinese men married and lived with Hawaiian women. Their children represented the first Chinese-Hawaiian generation, integrating traditions, foods, and customs of both cultures into their daily lives. Many Chinese-Hawaiian children, for instance, enjoyed both rice, a Chinese staple, and a traditional paste-like Hawaiian dish called poi.

Some men had two families; they married a Hawaiian but also had a Chinese wife living in the old country. The Chinese tradition of concubines and the Hawaiian tradition of plural marriages made this an acceptable arrangement on the islands. Sometimes wives and children came from China and lived with the Hawaiian family. One daughter of a Hawaiian mother living in such a household recalls,

> Our family is large. Father had eight children; four boys from the first wife [Chinese] and four girls from the second wife [Hawaiian]. All of us children called the first wife "mother" regardless of whose children we really were. The second wife we call "Jah" which in Chinese means "second mother." This seemingly strange family situation can be explained by the age-old Oriental custom which allows a man to have more than one wife. . . .
>
> Our family is closely integrated, and we all work for the welfare of the home. . . . However peculiar may have been the household situation, I

can say with sincerity that the happiness I found and the culture I received in my home are equal, if not superior, to the culture that could be got under any other family culture.[47]

Island Schools

Although California and other Western states banned Chinese young people from public schools, in Hawaii children of plantation laborers attended the local public schools. By the turn of the twentieth century, these schools taught workers' children the same curriculum and lessons that the plantation owners' sons and daughters received. Having more educational opportunities than children on the mainland, Chinese children in Hawaii often had higher expectations for future careers.

Their instruction led them to believe that a good education would lead to a better job, and Chinese parents hoped their children would do something more than labor in the cane fields. One young Chinese student declared at a conference in 1928, "You cannot force the Oriental youth with a high school education to go back to the plantations. He will not do it. We realize that our parents started on the plantations, but you cannot expect us to go back. I am an Oriental and I am speaking from the standpoint of the Oriental who has been educated."[48]

In addition to public education, Chinese Christian schools were organized by Episcopalian, Methodist, and Presbyterian missionaries. Hawaiian-born children of Chinese immigrants attended these religious schools in the evenings and on weekends in order to learn to read and write Chinese and to study traditional Chinese literature. Chinese Christian ministers were the first teachers in these schools, but later teachers came from China specifically to teach Chinese children the language and literary traditions of their ancestors.

Because immigrants were able to attend public schools and universities, they were able to enter the professional workforce earlier than their counterparts on the mainland. Both Hawaiian-born and immigrant Chinese became architects, accountants, chemists, dentists, engineers, lawyers, pharmacists, physicians, teachers—almost any occupation they desired. And, on the islands, they tended to face little discrimination.

Hawaii was a land of opportunity for many Chinese immigrants like this man who became a successful physician.

Hawaii: Land of Opportunity

From the beginning, even without an education, Chinese immigrants found opportunity in Hawaii. Many left the plantations and established small businesses of their own. They opened grocery stores or became peddlers or truck farmers; the most common business was to start a rice plantation and grow rice to sell.

In China, men had grown rice to feed their families, but in Hawaii they grew it to take to market. It required little investment. In general, they planted rice, harvested it, and found a ready sale, for Hawaiian farmers tried to meet the increasing demand for rice on the West Coast of the United States. (Chinese immigrants there wanted more than mainland farmers could produce.) Before long, Chinese immigrants had made rice the second most important source of income in Hawaii's economy; sugarcane was the first.

In 1882, missionary Frank Damon visited with the Chinese in Hawaii and described their work:

A few miles out from town [Honolulu] the rice plantations begin, and form a fringe bordering the shore for a long distance. This is the [spring] season for planting the rice, and the men are busy in the marshy fields from early morning till evening. The wide expanses lying at the foot of the valleys are just now beginning to be covered with tender shoots of rice, which in a few weeks will grow into a swaying luxuriant mass of verdure [green plants]. It requires a steady

Peddlers and Traders

Although rice was a profitable crop, many immigrants who lived in the countryside or on the outskirts of towns grew other crops to meet local demands. They introduced Chinese vegetables such as bok choy and soybeans and learned to produce Hawaiian favorites like bananas, taro, pineapples, and poi. Often, these small agricultural businesses grew as the Hawaiian economy expanded to meet the needs of its growing population.

Other immigrants started as rural peddlers or traders and over the years became urban shopkeepers, relying on bartering skills they had learned at home. One Hawaiian of Chinese descent explained how the Chinese immigrants managed to get in to the business:

Even though the Chinese emigrant has been a farmer, or a worker around the village, nearly every one of them [the Chinese immigrants] has had some experience at bargaining. . . . Peddling has been taken up as a sort of secondary occupation. Many of the families have little or no land [in China]. . . . Then they go overseas, many of them soon get into peddling and hawking. . . . The peddler gets a little money and buys a box of fruit, some peanuts, and then carries them around selling them. When he has been at it a while, and has saved some money, he gets a cart and increases his stock. Eventually he may set up a small shop.[50]

Early immigrants often used the money they made peddling to buy land. Later they became wealthy as realtors, land speculators, and businessmen. Businesses owned and run by immigrants in Hawaii included everything from taxi stands and service stations to poolrooms, dance halls, and office space rentals. The Chinese bought lots of buildings in Honolulu, and they operated stores or small factories. By the early twentieth century, many of these businesses prospered, and the islands' population increased.

An Early Sugar Maker

Although commercial sugar production was eventually developed by Americans, it was first attempted by pioneering Chinese. One early account tells of Wong Tze-Chun, the first Chinese sugar maker in Hawaii. Wong arrived on the Hawaiian island of Lanai in 1802. He brought with him a sugar mill and boiling pans. He set up operation and began to produce sugar. His stint there did not last long, however. Weather conditions proved unfavorable on Lanai that year, so Wong gave up his unsuccessful venture and returned to China.

Chinese farmers in Hawaii became skilled at producing a number of different crops, including pineapple, rice, sugarcane, and bananas.

The China Quarter

Although Hawaii was a multiethnic community that welcomed people from many countries, the Chinese in some ways led lives similar to those immigrants living on the mainland. Most Chinese in Hawaii eventually left the plantations or the countryside and moved into towns, for instance. And just as the greatest concentration of Chinese families on the mainland lived in San Francisco before the mid–twentieth century, most Chinese-Hawaiian families lived in Honolulu. In fact, by the 1930s, many of the Hawaiian-born Chinese were concentrated there, and the population of Chinese in Honolulu actually outnumbered those in San Francisco.

Honolulu's China quarter, though, differed greatly from the Chinatowns on the mainland. According to Glick,

There was never a time when this section was exclusively Chinese or when all Chinese in Honolulu lived there. Honolulu's Chinatown could be more accurately described as the nucleus [center] of the Chinese community—a place where the Chinese first concentrated and which continued to be a center of Chinese business and social

The Black Plague of Honolulu

In late 1899, Honolulu's Chinatown faced a near catastrophe following an outbreak of the plague. The Board of Health instigated a strict quarantine and called out the militia to surround the China quarter. Everyone inside was trapped; no one was allowed to leave. Twice each day, inspectors came and examined the sick. Whenever a case of plague was found, the building was evacuated.

In order to kill the germs that carried the disease, the practice of the day required people living near the victim to burn their clothing and household possessions and fumigate their building. Residents stripped down, took antiseptic baths, and got new clothes, before being hustled off to detention camps for the quarantine period.

Chinatown businesses suffered from lack of activity, but matters grew worse on January 20, 1900, when one of the sanitary fires burned out of control. Flames jumped up the church spire, and soon heavy smoke filled the air. Residents grabbed what they could and tried to flee Chinatown. But at the section's borders stood guards with bayonets ready to stop anyone who tried to escape the quarantine.

Afraid a riot might start, the city organized volunteers with weapons to lead the frightened crowd of more than six thousand to the Kawaiahao Church grounds for a temporary shelter. Soon, contributions of food, clothing, tents, and blankets arrived from people in the city. Honolulu carpenters came and worked night and day to erect temporary shelters.

When the quarantine ended and residents returned home, most found nothing among the ashes. Some were able to rebuild, but many poor and homeless had to rely on the Chinese Relief Society that collected funds for them and distributed rice twice a week.

---

life even after Chinese residences were dispersed throughout the city.[51]

Within Honolulu's Chinatown, a Chinese merchant's store was the center of most immigrants' social life. In addition to selling goods like firecrackers, incense, Chinese herbs, and food, the store offered immigrants a place to find others from their region. They met, sat down, talked, exchanged gossip, and at times picked up letters or goods sent from relatives. Men might sit for hours telling Chinese folktales. Usually, the owner lived on the premises and cooked for his patrons, often offering a bite to eat and a place to spend the night for someone visiting Honolulu from another island.

As Chinatown grew, its influence on the larger Hawaiian society did too. The multiethnic community adopted some Chinese tastes and lifestyles. One tradition the Chinese community brought to Hawaii was the ancient Chinese opera. During the 1870s, the Chinese built a theater in Honolulu, and the Cantonese opera remained the highlight of Chinese entertainment there for more than fifty years. Young, old, rich, even paupers—all attended the opera. These elaborate dramas, sometimes with hundreds of performers, went on for hours, describing Chinese history, both real and legendary. At times, firecrackers were ignited to help set the mood and scenes. Going to the theater remained an important event for Chinese families until the younger generation found more pleasure in watching movies than spending long hours at the opera. By the 1930s, the theater had closed.

Festivals and Fun

Before families came to Hawaii, when plantations were far from towns, men often felt isolated. For entertainment in the evenings and on Sundays, they played games and gambled; some smoked opium, and a few grew rowdy. After the women and children arrived, plantations sponsored programs on the plantation grounds such as sports events, music, dancing, and movies. Plantation owners gave families individual cottages and often donated land on which to build temples so that the immigrants could celebrate their traditional festivals.

The biggest festival was the Chinese New Year, and it was one of the most loudly and colorfully celebrated. Each year, the plantation workers took off the first day of the lunar calendar (a date that varies annually but usually falls in late January or early February) and decorated their temples with flags and their huts with colorful lanterns. Families dressed in new clothes and went to visit one another. They exchanged paper cards

A Chinese merchant offers a variety of goods for sale at his shop in Honolulu's Chinatown.

wishing each other good luck, and musicians made music. Throughout the day and into the night, Chinese New Year was punctuated by the explosion of firecrackers, as everyone reveled in the festivities.

On February 4, 1886, the *Daily Bulletin* described the New Year parade in Honolulu:

> The Chinese [Fire Engine] Company's decorations . . . consisted partly of the irrepressible and ubiquitous triangular yellow dragon flags. . . . A jolly Chinaman wearing an enormous mask representing the head of a lion, followed by some half-a-dozen [men] attendants bearing a gorgeous train representing the body and tail of the monster; standard bearers

carrying aloft banners and flags; companies of [men with] halberdiers [long weapons on handles], [and] trident [three-pronged spear] bearers, were features of the Chinamen's . . . turnout that created a furor of excitement, particularly among the small boys, all along the route of the procession.[52]

Societies and Associations

The immigrants brought other traditions to Hawaii too. Just as the Chinese immigrants to the continental United States set up tongs, *fongs,* and district associations, the Chinese in Hawaii had organizations to help the newly arrived immigrants. Hoong Moon societies, like the tongs of San Francisco, were

Revelers parade a large, colorful dragon through the streets of Honolulu during the annual Chinese New Year celebration.

established to help the Chinese immigrants survive in their new country. The Hoong Moon societies had many names, and they were located in the rural areas and small towns on various islands. Before 1900, when many Chinese still lived in the countryside, they served as the basis of the social and recreational life for rural Chinese and provided help in times of need.

As immigrants moved to cities, they found other organizations to fulfill their needs. In Honolulu, the United Chinese Society was first organized in 1884 by merchants, and it remained the major voice of the Chinese community for more than fifty years. When Hawaii became a U.S. territory in 1900 and the mainland's exclusion laws were applied to the islands, the United Chinese Society sent a white lawyer to Washington, D.C., to fight them. The society hoped to do two things. First, society members tried to convince authorities that the islands' Chinese should not come under the exclusion acts. The immigrants wanted to continue to have the freedom to travel back and forth to China with ease. Second, they wanted assurance that American laws against "contract labor" would be upheld in Hawaii. The U.S. government denied the first request; exclusion laws were extended to Hawaii. But the second request was granted, and thousands of Chinese workers were freed from their cane and mill contracts.

By the 1930s, a new organization, the Hawaiian Chinese Civic Association, had replaced the United Chinese Society. This association had a different focus; its members wanted to embrace the changing times. The Civic Association encouraged Chinese Americans to get involved in Hawaiian politics and take part in civic organizations. According to Char,

> The leadership of the Hawaiian Chinese Civic Association was in the hands of college graduates who had returned from the mainland in the United States. As Hawaii-born Chinese, they were American citizens but had faced discrimination on the mainland. . . . These students [had] met landlords and landladies near their college campuses who would not rent to them. [They] also met discrimination in entering local professions and occupations.

> Members of the Chinese Civic Association took political action and entered politics. . . . [By midcentury] American-born Chinese were blended into the broad spectrum of Hawaii's peoples. [From then on,] they [were] involved in politics as Democrats or Republicans. They became members in the PTA, Boy Scouts, Rotary, masons, Lions, and other non-ethnic organizations.[53]

The Association's encouragement had convinced Chinese Americans to integrate into the civic and service organizations of Hawaii.

Chinese immigrants to Hawaii found their resettlement easier than did immigrants to the mainland. Because of the islands' broader and earlier acceptance of ethnic differences, most immigrants were able to integrate into the mainstream community with ease. They found economic security and prosperity, and as a result became a part of the political and cultural life of nineteenth- and twentieth-century Hawaii.

CHAPTER SIX

A Turning Point

Despite years of discrimination in the workplace, in schools, and in communities across the nation, for those of Chinese ancestry, World War II and the years following became a turning point. Immigration laws had singled out the Chinese and kept them from coming to the United States during the late nineteenth and early twentieth centuries, but the war years brought the repeal of these laws and allowed changes in Chinese immigration. Housing, new fields of employment, and educational opportunities opened up to American Chinese, and for the first time, many felt they had found their place in the United States.

Trying to Gain Acceptance

By the 1920s and '30s, most young Chinese Americans had become fully "Westernized." Although many still spoke Cantonese at home with their parents, in school they dressed and spoke like their classmates. As with all immigrant children, they wanted to fit in, to be accepted as Americans, and to have all the privileges of citizenship.

Often, these young people, whose parents ran laundries, restaurants, and small businesses or worked in factories, attended college in the hopes of breaking away from the hard life their parents endured. They believed that a college education would give them the chance for a professional career or a skilled occupation. Most, though, found that the only employment available to them was in Chinatown, a result of long-standing prejudicial beliefs. Jade Snow Wong, for instance, graduated with honors from Mills College in California and was advised by her college employment office to look at "Chinese companies" for employment because American companies never hired those of Chinese heritage.

Pardee Lowe was another child of immigrants who had trouble finding a job.

When Lowe was thirteen, his father warned him of racism against Chinese Americans. The young man ignored his father, though, and looked for work as an office boy, applying to one company after another. Lowe recalled, "My jaunty self-confidence soon wilted. . . . Suspicion began to dawn [on me]. What had Father said? 'American firms do not customarily employ Chinese.' . . . I broke down and wept. For the first time I admitted to myself the cruel truth—I didn't have a 'Chinaman's chance.'"[54]

A Chinese student studies at a California college to become an aeronautical engineer. Even in the 1930s, Chinese Americans faced a great deal of racism when they sought employment outside of Chinatown.

Outsiders Even in Their Homeland

Although they tried hard to find good jobs and acceptance in American society, young Chinese Americans, even those born in the United States, were consistently viewed as outsiders or foreigners. "I realized very soon," said a young woman who moved from Hawaii to the mainland to attend college, "that I was not an American in spite of the fact that I had citizenship privileges. At the university, I was referred to as a *foreign* student; I objected to being called such at first; I insisted that I was an American—born on American soil and coming from an American . . . state. But soon, I learned that I was laughed at, mocked at my contention that I was an American and should be treated as such. . . . I gradually learned that I am a foreigner—a Chinese—

that it would be wiser to admit it and to disclaim my American citizenship."[55]

Experiences like these were common. American Chinese found that even if they spoke perfect English and dressed like their classmates, they could not blend in. They looked different and people treated them differently. Since they seldom found employment with American companies or in the public sector, young people were occasionally discouraged from attending college because of their Chinese ancestry. One college student recalled, "When I entered and registered, they [the staff at the college] told me very definitely that I could take [teaching] courses, but after the courses don't expect to be placed [in the public schools], because you are Chinese. [The registrar of San Francisco State College told me], I want you to understand this be-

Chinese American or American Chinese?

Because of the prejudice against them, Chinese Americans often found it hard to assimilate in America. Dr. Rose Hum Lee thought the Chinese could mix more easily if they changed their ways. Lee was an American of Chinese descent who became one of the top sociologists of her era. She researched Chinese living in America and was concerned because she felt those of Chinese heritage needed to better adapt to mainstream American culture.

One way to do this, Lee said, was to use a new term, *American Chinese,*

instead of the phrase *Chinese American.* Lee felt the old term seemed to emphasize the Chinese above the American, and that would mean, according to Lee, second-class citizenship.

During the 1950s, the term *American Chinese* was commonly used. But by the end of the twentieth century, many people used the term *Chinese American* or even *Asian American* to indicate those citizens whose ancestors came from any of a number of Asian countries, including China.

Chinese American soldiers give the victory salute the day after the Japanese attacked Pearl Harbor. Japan's attack caused America to join the fighting in World War II with China as an ally.

cause I don't want you to go through four years and find yourself disappointed."[56]

World War II

However, after the United States entered World War II, most Chinese Americans gained greater acceptance in American society. When the Japanese attacked Pearl Harbor on December 7, 1941, America quickly joined the fighting and one of the country's allies was China. Thus, people of Chinese descent were suddenly viewed with favor by most Americans and the news media.

For Chinese Americans, the war meant the chance to show their patriotism. Young men from Chinatowns across the country signed up for the military. Residents raised money by purchasing war bonds, and in New York, relatives and friends cheered as the first draft numbers drawn were those of Chinese Americans. Chinese women got involved in fund-raising efforts, blood donations, first aid, and refugee relief activities. Some even joined the Women's Army Corps (WAC), which helped the war effort without being involved in actual combat. Emily Lee Shek was the first Chinese American to join the WAC. According to the *Chinese Press* in 1942, "She [Shek] tried to join up right in the beginning [of the war], but the 105 pound weight minimum barred her. When the requirement was dropped five pounds, she drank two gallons of water and lived on a special Chinese diet, and made it—yes, with one pound to spare."[57]

For the young men and women who joined the armed forces, the opportunity to live outside Chinatowns and participate in a service to the United States was exciting. Charlie Leong, a Chinese American journalist, said, "To the men of my generation World War II was the most important historic event of our times. For the first time we felt we could make it in American society."[58]

By taking part in the fighting, American Chinese could show their loyalty to their country and feel like a part of American life. Harold Liu, who lived in New York's Chinatown, remembered,

> In the 1940s for the first time Chinese were accepted by Americans as being friends because at that time, Chinese and Americans were fighting against the Japanese and the Germans and the Nazis. Therefore, all of a sudden, we became part of an American dream. . . . It was just a whole different era and in the community we began to feel very good about ourselves.[59]

Some people also joined the war effort to defeat racism at home and to show that Asian Americans were true patriots. Kamin Chin explains this attitude: "My family had been here for over 100 years. I can't change the shape of my eyes. But I am an American. I was fighting discrimination."[60]

New Employment Opportunities

As the United States began to prepare for war in 1941, the National Association for

These Chinese welders, like many other Chinese Americans, worked hard for the war effort.

the Advancement of Colored People (NAACP) held demonstrations protesting racial discrimination in the defense industries. Shortly afterward, civil rights leaders went to Washington, D.C., to meet with President Franklin Roosevelt to demand that racial tolerance be practiced at home. Within a week, Roosevelt signed Executive Order 8802. It read, in part, "There shall be no discrimination in the employment of workers in defense industries or Government because of race, creed, color, or national origin . . . and it is the duty of employers and of labor organizations . . . to provide for the full and equitable participation of all workers in defense industries without discrimination."[61]

For minorities, this order meant an opportunity for better jobs, and American

Chinese now found all kinds of employment available to them. Manufacturing plants needed engineers, architects, and scientists in electronics and missile research. Chinese men and women with college degrees, who could get only menial jobs in the past, suddenly discovered the doors of employment thrown wide open.

Like other young American women, Chinese women took jobs building aircraft, riveting in the shipyards, running machine tools, and serving as secretaries in defense plants. College-educated Jade Snow Wong obtained employment as a typist/clerk in a shipyard in California. When her boss was promoted, he promoted her, too, and gave her a research and planning job. Finally, she held a position for which her degree had prepared her.

Chinese Entertainers

Opportunities for other Chinese Americans came in a variety of fields as the war economy expanded the jobs available to all Americans. One industry that grew during the war era was the entertainment industry. As Americans sought more and new modes of amusement, movies, nightclubs, and stage shows played to big audiences. In cities, Chinese American nightclubs opened and thrived. In San Francisco, the Forbidden City nightclub, with its own band and an all-Chinese cast of dancers, held audiences of twenty-two hundred a day during its boom years. Performing Western-style dancing and singing, Chinese entertainers at the Forbidden City and other clubs drew largely enthusiastic white audiences.

Alice Fong Yu, the First Chinese American Schoolteacher

Prejudice in the workplace kept many Chinese Americans from participating in various jobs, but Alice Fong Yu was determined to have the job she wanted—teaching elementary school.

Alice Fong was the second oldest of eleven children. In 1916, when Alice was about ten years old, her father moved his family to Vallejo, California, where he operated a grocery store. In Vallejo, Alice and her brothers and sisters attended the one-room schoolhouse with white students. Alice remembered experiencing prejudice as a child; the white students refused to hold her hand when they played games. Her parents told her to ignore those ill-behaved children, saying that if she worked hard she could go to college and get a job in China.

Alice studied hard and finally graduated from the San Francisco Teacher's College in 1926, but she had no intention of going to China to work. Instead, she convinced the San Francisco School District to hire her, and she became the first Chinese American teacher. She went to teach at the Commodore Stockton Elementary School, once called the Oriental Public School. Although Alice later married and had two sons, she taught for forty-four years until she retired in 1970.

Seeing Chinese Americans in roles traditionally reserved for white entertainers only broadened the appreciation and understanding of Chinese Americans. Mary Mammon, an entertainer at the Forbidden City, thought Chinese entertainers were popular because

"We were a novelty." . . . The white clientele was drawn to . . . orientals imitating Western song and dance. Surmising that Chinese American performers were Chinese nationals [Chinese citizens instead of Americans], some marveled that they could even sing in English. Others asked if they could touch them, not ever having seen real Chinese before.[62]

Changing Government Policies and Laws

As the public interacted more with American Chinese, popular opinion and government policies began to change, becoming more tolerant and accepting. Then, in a message to Congress on October 11, 1943, President Franklin Roosevelt asked for a repeal of the Chinese exclusion laws. The president said that such laws were undemocratic and the Chinese and other immigrants should be treated as Americans, complete with the rights and privileges of citizenship.

Before the end of the year, Congress responded, passing a bill that repealed all or part of each of the fifteen exclusionary laws enacted between 1882 and 1913. One of the most important repeals said that Chinese were no longer blocked from immigrating legally to the United States. Like other immigrants, Chinese then became part of an annual quota system based on national origin, the nation or country from which people emigrated. Each country was allowed a set number of people per year who could come as immigrants. Congress also amended the nationality act to allow persons of Chinese descent to be eligible for naturalization even if they were born in another country.

Even though Congress eliminated exclusion and gave supposed equality to Chinese immigrants, the country-of-origin law remained unfair. The government's National Origins Act favored northern and western Europeans and set no limits on Canadian and Mexican immigrants. Furthermore, the Chinese, with one of the world's largest populations, were given one of the smallest quotas at 105. In addition, a person of European parentage who wanted to immigrate could come to the United States through Canada and bypass the quota. A person of Chinese heritage who wanted to emigrate from Canada on the other hand, still fell under the "Chinese quota." Thus, despite the repeal of the exclusion laws, many believed American immigration laws were still designed to keep Chinese and other Asian immigrants to a minimum.

A Few Exceptions

Despite this, Congress did decide to reward the thousands of Chinese men who had fought for the United States in World War II. In 1945, Congress passed the War Bride Act and in 1946 the G.I. Fiancées Act. These laws allowed the fiancées, wives, and children of Chinese servicemen to immigrate to America without being included in the annual quota. As a result of these new acts, large numbers of Chinese women came to the United States for the first time in the country's history. From 1944 to 1953, more than 80 percent of the Chinese immigrants to America were women, and more than seven thousand of those came as war brides.

The government also allowed many Chinese professionals and students, who were trapped in the United States following the outbreak of the Second World War, to stay. In 1948, Congress passed the Displaced Persons Act, followed in 1952 by the McCarran-Walter, and in 1953 by the Refugee Relief Act. These laws all permitted Chinese, who might face danger in going home, to remain in the United States and gain citizenship.

Aside from these exceptions, the 105 Chinese quota lasted until the Immigration Act of 1965, which abolished the unjust national origin quotas. The new immigration law allowed 170,000 immigrants from the Eastern Hemisphere and 120,000 from the Western Hemisphere to immigrate to America each year. The law entitled 20,000 immigrants per country for the Eastern Hemisphere, including China, but husbands, wives, children, and parents of U.S. citizens were exempt from this quota. For those coming under the quotas, preference would be given to adults with relatives in the United States, those with valuable skills, artists, and refugees.

A New Kind of Immigrant

With the changing laws after World War II, a new wave of immigration began, and

These Chinese immigrants were among the first to arrive in America following passage of the 1953 Refugee Relief Act.

many, like Sez-Kew Dun, came with different expectations than previous immigrants. These newcomers planned to stay in the United States and hoped to find professional jobs. Dun was born in Canton and is typical of the Chinese who emigrated after the Second World War. She had an education and spoke Mandarin Chinese rather than the Cantonese of earlier entrants. She received her college degree from Xiangqin University of Guangdong in 1941 and wanted to continue her education, but the war in China prevented her from doing so. Eventually, Dun received a scholarship to study for a master's degree at the University of Oregon. Accepting the scholarship, she set out alone for Oregon. She says,

My life in Oregon was fun. Since my scholarship only covered my tuition, I had to support myself. A friend of mine introduced me to an American couple, Mr. and Mrs. Alvin C. Stockstads who operated an appliance store in Eugene. The Stockstads provided room and board for me, and in turn, I would work one hour a day to cook and to clean house for them. I never cooked in China and did not know how to cook in the beginning, but they taught me. They also showed me how to use a vacuum cleaner. [After a while] I treated them like my parents. . . . The friendship between us grew so strong that the Stockstads bought my wedding dress and airline ticket for my honeymoon when I got married.[63]

Some Things Change, Some Stay the Same

The type of immigrant was not all that changed. Many American Chinese returned from the war with a new sense of pride and confidence, feeling they had finally become part of American culture. The dwindling discrimination meant many could move outside Chinatown and find professional employment.

Despite these successes, though, many Chinese discovered that their ability to rise up to the highest professional levels remained blocked. One engineer explained, "We get steady positions as professional workers, with a steady, middle-class income. We'll get slight promotion, but after that subtle discrimination comes in." Others agreed that finding work to match their ed-ucation and skill level remained difficult. In fact, one writer said in professions "such as accounting, engineering, [and] computer programming which requires a high level of competence and accuracy, they [Chinese Americans] usually [were] kept from going one step further to the level where decisions are made."[64]

The Communist Threat

As Chinese Americans struggled to gain professional acceptance, a new concern emerged. In 1949, mainland China became a Communist government under the leadership of Mao Tse-tung. Following the end of World War II, the Soviet Union had established Communist governments in much of Eastern Europe, and many Americans feared that Communist ideology—an economic system that allowed for considerable government control over citizens' lives—would spread to the United States and other capitalist countries around the world. In 1950, responding to this widespread concern, Congress passed the Internal Security Act, which allowed the government to detain Communists who were deemed a threat to national security. As anti-Communist hysteria spread across the country, the U.S. government grew suspicious that some Chinese living in the United States might be working as agents of Communist China.

In Chinatowns around the nation, Chinese Americans responded to these fears by forming organizations like the All-American Overseas Chinese Anti-Communist League in New York and the Anti-Communists Committee for Free China. These groups declared their loyalty to the United States and opposed the ideals of communism. The Chinese Six Companies in San Francisco and the Chinese Consolidated Benevolent Association of New York also led campaigns to show that Chinese Americans were patriotic citizens. Association members wrote documents proclaiming their loyalty and hung these statements in shop windows in Chinatowns.

Despite these efforts, fear of communism continued, and the federal government began investigating thousands of Chinese Americans, having discovered that they had false papers and false birth certificates. As a result, many paper sons and daughters were deported, and thousands of Chinese in America grew uneasy. They protested, arguing that even though they had come to America illegally—a necessity, they often claimed—they were loyal citizens who believed in and supported America's democratic ideals.

In order to help investigate these claims, the government passed the Confessions System Act in 1957. This act allowed Chinese aliens and paper sons and daughters to come forward—to confess that they had immigrated illegally—so they could gain regular immigrant status and eventually legal citizenship. Some chose this option, but many Chinese did not. They remained afraid of the U.S. government; thousands of paper sons and daughters never confessed. Instead, they chose to keep their true identities a secret, sometimes even from family members and friends.

One paper son, Tung Pok Chin, who had been in the U.S. Navy during World War II, refused to take advantage of the confession law. His experiences with the U.S. government made him cautious. Once in the early 1950s, after mainland China had become a Communist country, two FBI agents had come to his laundry and started asking him

Immigration officials question Chinese immigrants suspected of being Communists. As anti-Communist hysteria spread across the United States, thousands of Chinese Americans were detained and questioned.

questions about his loyalty to the United States. "I could not help getting excited," he later wrote. "I felt they were trying to trick me into saying certain things, and that if I did not watch myself I could be manipulated into admitting to things that were not true. Already we had heard many instances of other paper sons and their families being deported."[65]

Joining the Mainstream Society

Questions of loyalty, professional inequality—these are some of the reasons that, despite all the successes Chinese Americans experienced in the years after World War II, some remained "unassimilated," isolated from the larger American community. Another reason is the desire of many within the Chinese American community to hold on tightly to their culture's ancient ideals and traditions. Sociologist Rose Hum Lee studied this phenomenon. Born in Butte, Montana, in 1904 and having received her doctorate in sociology from the University of Chicago in 1947, Lee wondered why the American Chinese had not assimilated better into mainstream American society. In 1960, she published a book, *The Chinese in the United States of America,* in which she contended that, for many Chinese Americans, assimilating also meant leaving their Chinese ways behind. Lee argued that such a steadfast desire to maintain the old was actually preventing many immigrants and their families from reaping the benefits of life in the United States. People could continue to eat Chinese foods and celebrate certain holiday traditions, she said, but they also had to look to American culture and traditions for their future.

Although much of the older generation disagreed with her, most of the younger generation applauded Lee's ideas. Finding their place in two cultures was sometimes confusing, but by the end of the 1960s, many young Chinese Americans believed that they needed to show pride in their unique Asian ancestry and, at the same time, be accepted as equal American citizens.

As a result, the Chinese American community began to join with other Asians, forming nationwide alliances. Asian Americans looked for ways to celebrate their heritage and increase their visibility in American society. Through their efforts, President Ronald Reagan signed a bill in 1988 calling for Asian Pacific American Heritage Week, and President Bill Clinton proclaimed Asian Pacific American Heritage Month starting in May 1993. Asians also banded together to explore their common roots in organizations such as the Association of Asian/Pacific American Artists, the Asian American Theatre Company, Asian Americans in Higher Education, Asian American Journalists, and even local groups such as the Asian Law Caucus of San Francisco.

The advent of such groups and other achievements in the years during and after World War II brought new opportunities and new challenges for those of Chinese lineage. While fighting for equality and democracy overseas, America emerged from the war with a new sense of justice, allowing Chinese Americans a chance for advancement and progress in American society.

CHAPTER SEVEN

Living in Two Worlds

The cultural traditions the early immigrants brought with them helped make their new surroundings feel less strange. They clung to their habits of dress, worship, festivals, and celebrations. Maintaining these traditions made adjusting to life on the American frontier and the islands of Hawaii easier. These pioneers built altars and temples, celebrated Chinese festivals, told their folktales and stories, played traditional music, and handed down folk medicine and herbal cures.

But by the early twentieth century, the younger generation thought many of their family and Chinese traditions were old-fashioned. As a result, many of the second generation found themselves struggling to blend the ideals and practices of two different worlds. Many felt they had one foot in their Chinese world and another in their American world. As one young American of Chinese ancestry wrote, "We occupy a most unique position standing betwixt the cultures and traditions of our forefathers and the land of our birth."[66]

Worshiping, Building Temples, and Music

The beliefs and practices of ancient Chinese thrived in America as the earliest arrivals to mining and logging towns built

Chinese Medicine

Chinese immigrants brought Oriental medicine with them when they came from China. This health care practice had been in use for more than three thousand years, and treatments included herbal medicines, diet, massage, meditation, acupuncture, and exercise. The therapies use physical energies believed to exist in all living things to encourage the body to heal itself.

Oriental medicine is based on the idea of body energy rather than on the biochemical practices of modern Western medicine. The vital energy in all life processes was called *Qi* (pronounced "chee") by the ancient Chinese physicians. *Qi* circulates through the body along certain routes, and each route is associated with specific physiological systems of the body's organs. People get sick, say Chinese doctors, because of imbalances of *Qi* in the body. The doctor's job is to restore the balance of *Qi* within the body, using intricate systems of pulse and tongue analysis and the patient's symptoms to determine a diagnosis and a cure.

Today, Oriental medicine continues to treat about 25 percent of the world's population. And many people in the United States (Asian and not) seek health improvements using some of the methods first brought to America by Chinese immigrants.

Taoist and Buddhist temples for worship and celebrations. Many early temples looked like log cabins, for the men used the materials available on the frontier. Later temples, however, more closely resembled pagodas in China. During the 1850s, for instance, Chinese miners in Marysville, California, built the first Bok Kai temple soon after their arrival. In the spring of 1869, the small temple was moved to a brick building and later rebuilt by the Sze Yup Hiu Kuan association to look more like a traditional Chinese temple. Today, it still stands along the north bank of the Yuba River and remains a place of celebration.

The religious practices within the temples—making offerings and prayer, for instance—were basically the same. The Marysville temple and others like it generally contained a figure of some deity, most often Kwan Gung, who represents justice and divine protection. There was no particular day of the week for services, and prayers could be said whenever the temples were open. A worshiper bowing before the altar often brought incense and made an offering and a request of the gods. As Tin-Yuke Char explains,

> In following their religious traditions the Chinese in Hawaii went to the temples of their choice two or three times a year to offer thanks for divine protection and good fortune, or at times of a family crisis such as sickness. . . .

Simple, private ceremonies at home were held on occasional festival days. . . . The oldest and most frequented of the various Chinese temples in Honolulu is the Goon Yum (Kwan Yin) Temple or the Goddess of Mercy Temple on Vineyard Street. Established first in the early eighties [1880s] they are still used.[67]

Many people today maintain these ancient traditions and practices. As sociologist Rose Hum Lee says,

The average Chinese is thus a religious . . . [mixture]. He is at one and the same time a Confucianist, Taoist and Buddhist. For example a Chinese worships his ancestors to demonstrate his belief in filial piety [respect for elders], a virtue upheld by Confucian ethics. This is practiced in the home through ritualistic observances in front of ancestral tablets [small altars]. . . . Rituals revolve around the offering of sustenance items: wine, rice, meat, fowls, paper money, paper clothing. . . . Candles light the way for the ancestors to come forward and partake of the food. Incense blurs the vision of the evil spirits. . . . [At temples] to make certain the ancestors hear what

Kong Chow Buddhist Temple in San Francisco's Chinatown is one of many Buddhist and Taoist temples in America built by Chinese immigrants.

the worshippers say, Buddhist as well as Taoist priests clang cymbals and gongs to ensure that the supplications of the living are heard and answered in the ancestral world.[68]

Besides following these Eastern religious practices, Chinese immigrants to the United States also sometimes worshiped among the various Christian sects. Some immigrants accepted these faiths as their only church, but for others the long-standing Chinese tradition of following many beliefs allowed them to both continue their more traditional rites and accept Christianity.

Early immigrants also brought to America their love of music and their musical instruments. They carried stringed instruments, reed instruments, bells, cymbals, and gongs. In mining and logging camps, Chinese music often floated in the air during idle hours. According to Liping Zhu, "After a full day or season of mining activities, the Chinese enjoyed native music, playing oriental instruments or singing Canton opera. Imported instruments included moon guitars, bamboo flutes, Chinese violins, vertical flutes, drums, gongs, and cymbals."[69]

Women dressed in traditional Chinese costumes celebrate the Chinese New Year in San Francisco in the 1930s. Later generations became less interested in preserving the Chinese traditions.

New and Old Generations

Even though maintaining these traditions worked well for the first immigrants, as their children grew up, the younger generation was less interested in preserving the old ways. Teenagers especially wanted to do the same activities as their non-Chinese classmates. Remembering his years growing up in San Francisco, an American of Chinese descent explained,

> By the time I was in high school, the big thing, if you had money was to have a car. Then a girl. You would have to dress fairly well, not in dress-up clothing but in sports clothing. My father wouldn't give us any money for working in the store, but we did get an allowance, and I'd use that to try to get the right clothes.[70]

Children also began questioning their parents' values and ideals, which differed from those of their American teachers and classmates. Their objections became stronger as they visited American homes. Jade Snow Wong worked as a housekeeper for a Caucasian family and she was amazed at how the members of that family related to one another.

> It was a home where children were heard as well as seen; where parents considered who was right or wrong, rather than who should be respected; where birthday parties were a tradition, complete with lighted birthday cakes, where husband kissed his wife and the parents kissed their children; . . . and where, above all,

Children born to Chinese American immigrants often challenged their parents' values and ideals.

each member, even down to and including the dog appeared to have the inalienable right to assert his individuality—in fact, where that was expected—in an atmosphere of natural affection.[71]

Girls and Boys

Besides respecting individual rights, it seemed most Americans also gave as much importance to girls as to boys. Chinese convention, on the other hand, considered male children more valuable because they carried on the family name. Thus, the birth of a son was cause for the gathering of family and friends. Once a boy grew to manhood, he had more authority and respect in the Chinese family than any woman.

Jade Snow Wong was one Chinese American woman who felt frustrated as she tried to reconcile these Chinese practices. She questioned the idea that fathers were always right and that boys were always more important than girls. Wong had grown up always accepting her father's word as final until he refused to pay for her college education because she was a woman, and he had no funds for her. Wong writes,

Daddy had spoken. He returned to his Chinese paper with finality and clamped on his glasses again. By habit, [I] questioned aloud no more. . . . But [my Americanized] mind was full of questions. . . . [I thought] I can't help being born a girl. . . . I don't want to marry, just to raise sons! Perhaps I have a right to want more than sons! I am a person, besides being a female. Don't the Chinese admit that women also have feelings and minds?[72]

Despite Wong's and others' protests, the old ideas persisted. Because boys held superior positions in traditional Chinese society, in America they were often given more privileges than their sisters; boys could leave their homes without permission and had more educational opportunities. Although mothers and fathers saw this as acceptable, their daughters felt it was unequal treatment. "I am American-born of Chinese parentage, and because of my American training I feel the restraints imposed by the Chinese traditions," said Lillie Leung, a Chinese American living in Los Angeles.

I feel the restrictions imposed upon the girls: we are not permitted to go out to socials or to have good times as the American girls have. . . . I have wanted to work—just do any kind of work to feel that I was doing something and making my own way—but my parents would not listen to it because it might appear that they could not support their children. . . . My parents wanted to hold to the old idea of selecting a husband for me, but I did not care for them and would not marry them.[73]

In some cases, boys and girls agreed that the old ways were unacceptable. Both genders tended to reject their parents' views on dating and marriage, for instance. Chinese custom said it was the parents' responsibility to choose someone suitable for their son or daughter to marry. This was often arranged through a go-between, usually an older woman who found an acceptable marriage partner for the son or daughter of a family. The candidate had to have certain qualifications to be considered as a bride or groom. A woman might be acceptable if she were pretty, refined, or could work hard. A man had to have a good job, a promising future, or come from a village near the family's home in China. American-born young people rebelled against these ideas, however. They wanted to choose their own husbands or wives, based on the ideal of romantic love and companionship.

Clash of Views

As the Chinese traditions and customs became more and more confining, youngsters clashed with their parents about dating, curfews, friends, music, how to spend money, attending Chinese schools, and even American educational traditions. Most parents, for instance, valued education, long respected in Chinese tradition. For most parents, though, it was more important for the son to go on to college than the daughter. Jade Snow Wong's father finally said she could have a college education, but he refused to help her pay for it. He told her,

> You are quite familiar by now with the fact that it is the sons who perpetuate our ancestral heritage by permanently bearing the Wong family name and transmitting it through their blood line, and therefore the sons must have priority over the daughters [in getting a good education]. . . . Our daughters leave home at marriage to give sons to their husbands' families to carry on the heritage for other names.[74]

In spite of her father's objection, Jade Snow Wong and others like her asserted their independence. Wong started off at a junior college and soon got a scholarship to help with her college expenses. Others found jobs their Chinese parents disapproved of such as being dancers, musicians, or entertainers. Some took new names that sounded more American. With a Chinese name like Mei Guen, a young woman would call herself Mae Gwen, or

Chinese American college students dance at a fraternity party. Many children of Chinese immigrants ignored their parents' objections and adopted American values and customs.

a young man with a name like Wei Lim would introduce himself as William. For many young people, it was a struggle to figure out where they belonged and which part of their heritage they should follow.

Family Celebrations

With the passing years, customs changed and families adapted. Traditions such as arranged marriages gradually faded as the second generation grew more and more Westernized. There were some traditions, though, that changed little or not at all. Family celebrations commemorating births, marriages, and deaths, for instance, were slow to change. These traditions seemed important to maintain, for they were part of a large ancestral Chinese cul-

ture that had been preserved for more than two thousand years.

The celebration after the birth of a child was one custom the Chinese continued to follow in the new country. In China, babies were born at home, and for most immigrant families, even into the twentieth century, a baby would be born at home with a midwife. Many immigrants continued to distrust Western medicine or were denied access to white hospitals. The midwife was given a fee for her services and also *li shee* (money wrapped in red paper) in celebration of the great event.

After the arrival of an infant, the extended family prepared special food. In Chinatowns across America, the smell of pig's feet boiled in vinegar and ginger announced that a new baby had been born. No one remembered the ancient signifi-

Longevity Banquets

Longevity banquets or special birthday parties are a common practice among those of Chinese ancestry. Since the elderly are greatly revered in Chinese culture, a special festival is given to those who have reached an advanced age such as seventy-five or eighty years old.

In place of ice cream and cake, longevity banquets offer Chinese foods served in several courses. These might include boiled chicken, barbecued squabs, roast ducks, seafood, diced meats and vegetables, dumplings stuffed with crushed almonds, black soybeans, peanuts, shredded coconut, and Chinese pudding cakes made with either rice flour and brown sugar or taro flour and sesame seeds. Good friends, relatives, and business associates are invited, and there are tributes made to the celebrated person. A family may spend weeks in preparation for this great event honoring the elderly parent or grandparent. When the evening is over, a rice bowl and pair of chopsticks are commonly given to each guest to take home. These favors are a way of wishing the guests a long life and a good future.

cance of this practice, but female family members knew the nutritional value for the new mother was important. Family and friends also dyed eggs red to celebrate the birth and often delivered the eggs, along with slices of roast pork and pickled ginger and stuffed buns, to friends who brought gifts for the newborn.

As the years passed and this practice changed, immigrants began having two "eggs and ginger" parties for the baby, usually when he or she is one month and one year old. These gatherings include anything from a full nine-course banquet to a more simple meal, depending on the family's ideas and circumstances. Guests and relatives bring *li shee* even today, using special red envelopes.

Weddings and Funerals

When the Chinese celebrate, red is the primary color for the festivities because it symbolizes good luck and happiness. Thus, a bride traditionally dressed in red for her wedding. Today, though, most brides of Chinese ancestry wear white. Sometimes, women put on red heirloom jackets over white gowns. Many brides also follow conventional American rites. Some walk up an aisle to music while others just say their vows in front of family or friends.

Weddings during the early twentieth century were often a blend of old Chinese traditions and new American practices. In describing marriage customs in Hawaii in the 1930s, Char writes,

The arrival of the bride is heralded with a blast of firecrackers [an old

Most modern Chinese American brides wear a white, rather than a traditional red, bridal dress.

Chinese tradition]. The marriage is then performed according to conventional Western wedding rituals. The [Chinese] custom of retiring and changing into a new dress to serve tea and candied fruits to friends and relatives still holds, and the friends may in return offer *li shee*. A feast usually precedes the wedding ceremony to which friends and relatives are invited. Only the bride attends this, as the [American] custom of forbidding the groom to appear [forbidding the groom to see the bride before the wedding] is still valid. The [Chinese] custom of segregating women and men by tables is still practiced.[75]

Another important ritual for Chinese families was the performance of a proper burial for the dead. The dead were supposed to be buried in ancestral burial grounds, where the deceased's spirit could rest in peace among other family members. In the early days, whenever possible, the bones of the deceased were returned to China to be buried alongside his ancestors. Sometimes, a person was first temporarily buried in the United States and later exhumed and returned to the homeland. By 1900, though, this practice generally stopped, but the selection of an auspicious burial plot in American cemeteries remains important for many.

Other funeral practices remained intact, though. In China, the wealthier the individual, the more elaborate the burial, and this continued in America. Immigrants also usually observed the traditional Chinese period of mourning, placing the body on view in the home for three days and nights before the funeral. Friends and family then kept a constant vigil before taking the body to be buried. After the vigil, a funeral procession took the deceased to the cemetery.

The funeral procession may have displayed Chinese images to keep away evil spirits, an ancestral tablet for the soul, and a large portrait of the deceased. "Spirit money" (fake money to distract evil spirits) was usually thrown along the route to keep the soul from being snatched by evil spirits before it could be buried. At the gravesite, clothing and other personal items were often burned to allow the departed soul to have its necessities in the afterlife. In the cemetery, feasting took place and special meatless dishes were served. In Hawaii, cubes of brown sugar were given out to help take away the bitterness of the occasion. Sometimes money was given for the same reason.

These customs changed over the years to fit American life, but the intent remains the same. Family members dress in white, the Chinese color of mourning. At the gravesites, spirit money is often burned in trash cans. Feasting is less common, but food is still placed as an offering at the cemetery.

Chinese New Year

Another way Chinese immigrants blended Eastern and Western traditions was by introducing their culture's festivals to their new country. All Chinese festivals have deep roots dating back more than five thousand years to the establishment of the lunar calendar. In their new home, the immigrants clung to the festivals of the lunar year, and over time altered them to blend with American traditions.

The biggest festival of the lunar calendar is the New Year, which falls between the winter solstice and the spring equinox, usually between late January and early February. According to legend, on the twenty-fourth day of the twelfth month, the kitchen god in each home leaves the earth to go to heaven and report on the behavior of the family. To please the kitchen god and to make certain his words in heaven were sweet, Chinese families burned paper money or joss (fortune) sticks or made offerings of wine and food. They also set off firecrackers to frighten away the demons that tradition said were afraid of light, red, and noise. And to get rid of any bad luck from the past year, Chinese houses were thoroughly swept and cleaned on the day before the New Year began.

In keeping with these practices, the earliest immigrants of the 1850s celebrated the Chinese New Year. Most immigrants thoroughly cleaned and sometimes decorated their houses, huts, barracks, or camps. They left offerings to the kitchen god, and on the first day of the new year, took time off work, usually visiting friends and relatives, dressed in their best clothes and sharing Chinese tea, melon seeds, tobacco, and candied fruits. Immigrants often exchanged small cards or oranges for good luck. And, of course, they also blasted firecrackers to keep away evil spirits.

Today, Chinese New Year is observed in a variety of ways. A Chinese home is often cleaned, and special foods such as sweet dumplings are prepared as relatives and friends gather to eat a special meal on New Year's Day. Sometimes new clothes are purchased for the event. And adults often give children red envelopes filled with money or candy.

Chinese New Year has become a well-known part of mainstream America and continues to be commemorated in towns and cities across the nation. On this holiday, the streets of San Francisco and New York are filled with loud and colorful celebrations. Firecrackers and rockets light up the sky and crackle in the night. There are theatrical performances and dragon dances, in which people parade down the street covered with a large mask head and cloth-body costume to represent a dragon. The pageantry of these events draws large crowds, as many Americans enjoy the Chinese New Year.

Other Holidays and Festivals

In addition to Chinese New Year, there are many other festivals celebrated by people of Chinese heritage. One of these is the Moon Festival. On the fifteenth day of the eighth month in the lunar calendar—the end of September—the Moon Festival arrives.

Fireworks explode during the Chinese New Year celebration in San Francisco in 1880.

The Moon Festival, sometimes called the Harvest Festival or moon's birthday, is, according to Chinese legend, when the moon is farthest from the earth and appears bright and perfectly round. During this time, moon cakes are made with flour and sugar and decorated to look like the moon. For most people of Chinese heritage, it is an important holiday. The Chinese Historical and Cultural Project website compares the Moon Festival to the "American Thanksgiving, an annual family get together [for Chinese Americans]."[76]

The early Chinese also brought the tradition of dragon dance, which is performed to ask for rain from the dragon spirit. The yearly dragon parade in Marysville, California, is billed as "California's Oldest Parade," although most of its significance remains unknown to the large crowds it draws each year. And in San Jose, California, the tradition of the dragon parade was revived on July 30, 1995. For the first time since 1924, after an interruption of seventy-one years, it once again became part of the annual celebrations in the city.

Even as young people pushed for the acceptance of American ideals and shunned antiquated Chinese customs, they held on to the traditions brought across the ocean by the first immigrants that made them Chinese. By introducing festivals, birth and death ceremonies, and wedding rituals to the larger American public, the Chinese Americans, whether first or second generation, have managed to exist with a foot in both worlds, blending that which makes them unique with newer Western traditions to create a distinctive, integrated culture.

CHAPTER EIGHT

Changing Patterns

D espite the exclusion laws and the discrimination of the early years of Chinese immigration, Chinese Americans today flourish in the United States. The descendants of immigrants live and work in every section of the country and make contributions in almost every field of American life.

Chinatowns: Golden Ghettos

Immigrants as well as citizens of Chinese heritage have helped to preserve America's Chinatowns, especially in places like New York and San Francisco. These Chinatowns remain vigorous centers of Chinese culture.

In San Francisco, heirlooms, old treasures, artwork, and crafts from China can be found, and parades, festivals, and cultural activities enliven the streets.

Businesses thrive in these city sections. Although many entrepreneurs no longer live where they work, Chinatowns provide services that draw shoppers, diners, tourists, and people wanting Chinese products. To those unfamiliar with Chinese lifestyles, they seem like fascinating places to see new sights and eat new foods without leaving the country.

These areas are also home to members of the older generation and many of the newly arrived immigrants who look for a way to make the new country feel less foreign. The older generation often prefers to remain in Chinatown, where they can hear and speak Chinese and where they have lived most of their lives. For new immigrants, some of whom live below the poverty line, government programs in Chinatowns provide housing, health care, educational opportunities, and schools for people in need.

Most middle-class Chinese Americans, though, live outside Chinatowns. "In actuality," writes Betty Lee Sung, "only a small percentage of the Chinese now live in Chinatowns. Most have successfully found their niches in the larger American society."[77]

Contributions and Achievements

Chinese Americans have woven their lives into American culture and inserted their talents into such diverse areas as the arts, business, architecture, education, sports, music, sciences, engineering, and medicine. Often, having an understanding of both their Chinese and American heritage has enhanced their ability to gain prominence in their chosen field. At other times, their individual desires and talents bring them distinction.

Constance Yu Hwa Chung, better known as Connie Chung, is one who used her own talent to find success. She became the second woman and the first Chinese American to appear on TV as a news anchor for a major national broadcasting firm. Chung, born in the United States to immigrant parents, was raised in Maryland outside Washington, D.C. As a child, she dreamed of being a ballerina but changed her mind by the time she began college at the University of Maryland. While still in college, she worked at WTTG-

What Kind of Athletes?

Early Chinese immigrants in America had little time to become athletes. With most of their hours spent making a living, few immigrants or their children had the opportunity to excel at sports. As Chinese Americans moved into the middle class, though, many have become athletic stars.

The 1980s and '90s found the descendants of Chinese immigrants making big news in athletic competitions. Tennis great Michael Chang, at just seventeen years old, was the youngest player ever to win the French Open, one of the major world tournaments. Americans cheered his victory as he became the first U.S. man to win the title in thirty-four years.

At the 1984 Olympics, Tiffany Chin took fourth place for women's figure skating. A few years later, Michelle Kwan's grace on the ice won her both admiration and medals as she skated in national and international competitions, including the Olympic Games. At the age of thirteen, Kwan earned a place as an alternate on the 1994 U.S. Olympic team. Four years later at the 1998 Winter Olympics, she won the silver medal.

TV, and in 1969 she graduated with a degree in journalism. Chung made her way up to reporter, and in 1973 was hired by CBS as a news correspondent.

Chung was determined to prove that Chinese American women could be successful in TV journalism, and she worked long hours to file the best reports. In 1976, she was given the job of news anchor at the CBS affiliate in Los Angeles, and in 1993 she accepted the coanchoring position with Dan Rather on the *CBS Evening News,* a position she held for two years. For a while, she also hosted her own weekly newsmagazine, *Eye to Eye with Connie Chung.* For her investigative reports and interviews, she won three Emmys and numerous other awards.

By 1994, Connie Chung had reached the top of her profession and was an inspiration to both women and Chinese Americans. But she was not satisfied. She was disappointed that national network evening news shows failed to keep women in nightly anchor spots. In 1997, she told a reporter for the *Boston Globe,* "Women, on air as reporters and anchors, outnumber men in local TV stations. . . . The [national] networks are still in the dark ages [for failing to keep women as news anchors on the evening programs]."[78]

Literature and Music

Others who garnered fame and brought prestige to Chinese American women include authors such as Amy Tan, Maxine Hong Kingston, and Ruthanne Lum McCunn. These women wrote best-selling novels that helped describe the lives of Chi-

Connie Chung, an Emmy award–winning television news anchor, is a role model for many Chinese Americans.

nese Americans. Tan's books include popular novels such as *The Joy Luck Club, The Hundred Secret Senses,* and *The Kitchen God's Wife,* which tell about the varying outlooks and lives of different generations of Chinese. Hong Kingston's highly acclaimed memoirs, *The Woman Warrior* and *China Men,* are the most widely taught books on college campuses by a living American author. And fictionalized biographies by McCunn describe legendary Chinese immigrants such as Polly Bemis and Lue Gim Gong. Tan's book *The Joy*

Laurence Yep

Chinese American author Laurence Yep was born in San Francisco in 1948 and grew up there. After high school, he attended Marquette University in Wisconsin and had his first story published in a science fiction magazine called *Worlds of If.* In 1970, he returned to California and soon graduated from the University of California at Santa Cruz with a master's degree in literature. Yep kept writing, and also went on to the University of New York at Buffalo to earn his Ph.D.

Yep has written historical fiction, science fiction, short stories, novels, picture books, and plays, but he is best known for his children's books. Yep's book *Dragonwings* won the Newbery Honor in 1976 and is based on a man named Fung Joe Guey who in 1910 built a biplane by hand and flew it for twenty minutes over the hills of Oakland, California. *Dragonwings* earned several other awards, and in the 1980s Yep adapted it to a stage play. The play was performed in Lincoln Center in New York and in the Kennedy Center in Washington, D.C. Yep's other Newbery Honor award book, *Dragon's Gates,* tells the story of a young boy who comes from China to help his father and uncle work on the Central Pacific Railroad.

In 1998, Yep published *The Rainbow People,* a collection of several Chinese folktales retold by the author. Three years later, he produced a second collection of folktales, *Tongues of Jade.* A talented and prolific writer, Laurence Yep enriches the field of literature with his many fine works.

Luck Club and McCunn's *A Thousand Pieces of Gold* have both been made into movies.

Chinese American men have also shown their literary talent. Perhaps the best-known playwright and screenwriter of Chinese descent is David Henry Hwang. His Tony Award–winning play *M. Butterfly* excited audiences around the world and was made into a movie by Warner Brothers. With several other works in music, for the stage, and on film, Hwang continues to find success with pieces about immigrants, Chinese, and Chinese Americans as well as works that have almost nothing to do with ethnic life. Hwang's accomplishments represent the richness of both his American and his Chinese heritage.

In music, too, Chinese Americans have found ways to bring together both their American and Chinese cultural traditions. From the beginning of their years in America, immigrants played traditional instruments and sang folk songs. During the twentieth century, Chinese immigrants and their children or grandchildren gained wide reputations with sounds from jazz to classical music.

Yo-Yo Ma, the son of immigrant Chinese musicians, is one of the most famous musicians in the world. He was just six years old when he first appeared on stage in Paris, playing his cello. Today he travels the world giving concerts, making albums, and espousing strong belief in music as a way to improve communication. "It allows you to express what your inner vision of something is,"[79] he recently told a reporter.

Ma is a man whose life and work have been influenced by his cross-cultural background. During the late 1990s, he established the Silk Road Project to help increase the understanding of the cultural traditions linking Asia and Europe. The Silk Road was the historic trade route that connected East and West during the seventh and eighth centuries. Musical instruments and techniques traveled along this road, leaving their impressions on the cultures they encountered. Ma's Silk Road Project brings together musicians and artists from places such as Mongolia, Iran, Azerbaijan, China, and Japan. Ma calls this project "a metaphor for what is possible today. If we take the most talented people [around the world] in artistic disciplines . . . we [can] make traditional things and innovative things work together."[80]

Art

Although Ma is reaching to bring Eastern and Western arts together, many visual artists with Chinese backgrounds found success in the United States by adopting Western techniques and materials. Yun Gee, a refugee from Canton, painted in the 1930s and '40s with artists like Georgia O'Keefe. Today, Gee is considered part of the modernist school of art, a collection of nineteenth- and twentieth-century artists who tried to reflect social and intellectual issues in their work. Despite his talent and education, Gee still faced some prejudice. Although his paintings were shown in many well-known galleries, he struggled to overcome the industry's scorn of Chinese painters and to be known as an artist rather than just as an Oriental from Chinatown.

Other artists like potter Jade Snow Wong combined traditions of their Chinese heritage with those they learned in American art studios. Wong integrated what she was taught by American potters with ancient Chinese pottery styles to create her own technique. She used a potter's wheel to form

Born to Chinese immigrants, cellist Yo-Yo Ma has become one of the most famous musicians in the world.

her pots, but then decorated them using both American and Chinese techniques.

Whether visual artists used traditional Western art styles or combined those with Eastern art methods, many more Chinese American artists are finding recognition for their work than they did in the past. Sculptor and architect Maya Lin, for instance, received wide acclaim for her work as the designer of the most visited public monument in the United States; she is the creator of the nationally celebrated Vietnam Veterans' Memorial in Washington, D.C. In addition, Lin designed the civil rights memorial in Montgomery, Alabama, commemorating those who lost their lives in the fight for racial equality. Both works include the names of participants in the events they honor, and both monuments elicit deep emotional responses from the people who view them.

Nobel Prize Winners

Many Chinese Americans have made significant contributions in the sciences too. The Nobel Prize is given each year to top scientists worldwide who make new discoveries, and three Chinese immigrants have been so honored.

Tsung Dao Lee and Chen Ning Yang were born in China, and they first met while they were students at the National Southwest Associated University in China. Both

Maya Lin: Designer of the Vietnam Veterans' Memorial

The most visited public monument in the United States, the Vietnam Veterans' Memorial, was designed by a Chinese American college student. Maya Lin was in her senior year at Yale University, majoring in architecture, when she submitted an entry to the competition for selecting the model for a memorial to be built in Washington, D.C.

Lin's proposal included designs for two long, low black-granite walls meeting to form a "V." Inscribed on those walls would be the names of the fifty-eight thousand dead or missing-in-action Vietnam War veterans. Although some veterans protested allowing someone of Asian descent to create a Vietnam War veterans' memorial, on May 6, 1981, Lin's design was chosen from 1,420 entries. On November 13, 1982, after a forty-eight-hour vigil in the Washington Cathedral, the memorial was dedicated.

Maya Lin was born in Ohio on October 5, 1959; both her parents had emigrated from China during the 1940s. After the Vietnam Veterans' Memorial was built, Lin returned to school and eventually received a master's degree and Ph.D. from Yale. She continues to work on various projects using her skills as both a sculptor and an architect.

came to the United States for advanced studies. Yang received his Ph.D. in 1948 from the University of Chicago, and two years later Lee received his Ph.D., also from the University of Chicago. In 1957, Lee and Yang brought great recognition to the Chinese American community when they were awarded the Nobel Prize in physics. And in 1976 Samuel Chao Chung Ting also received a Nobel Prize for physics.

Perhaps as a result of these prestigious accomplishments, other Americans of Chinese descent have continued to seek careers and degrees in sciences and engineering. Although Chinese students in general attend college in higher percentages than their white counterparts, they represent the highest percentage of any ethnic group enrolled in college science and engineering programs. In 1985, Asian Americans, including Chinese, received about 75 percent of all Ph.D. degrees in science and engineering, and by 1995 that had increased to 85 percent.

Chinese Americans Enter Politics and Civil Service

As those of Chinese ancestry attained prominence in the arts and sciences, they also began to win political offices and to take an active part in the political life of their nation and their community. The changes after World War II allowed Chinese Americans to seek positions in civic groups, service committees, boards of education, and local and national politics.

In 1959, Hawaii became the first state to send a Chinese American to the U.S. Senate. That year, Hiram Fong was elected to Congress, where he spent three terms be-

Professors Chen Ning Yang (rear, left) and Tsung Dao Lee pose with their wives after receiving the 1957 Nobel Prize in physics.

fore retiring in 1977. Before going to Washington, D.C., Fong had served in the Hawaiian Territorial Legislature from 1938 to 1954. Fong worked hard for Hawaii's admission to statehood and held the office of vice president of the Hawaiian state constitutional convention in 1950, the meeting during which the state of Hawaii wrote its constitution. Like so many others, Fong grew up the son of an immigrant sugar plantation worker, and his achievements brought great satisfaction and pride to the Chinese American community.

Almost forty years after Fong was elected to Congress, Gary Locke became the first Chinese American governor in U.S. history, winning election in Washington state on November 5, 1996. Governor Locke was born in 1950 to an immigrant family and spent his childhood in a Washington state government housing project provided for World War II veterans and their families. Eventually he attended undergraduate school at Yale University and obtained a law degree from Boston University before returning home. In 1982, he began his political career when he was elected to the Washington State House of Representatives.

Governor Locke has become well-known for his high regard for working people; he has proposed legislation aimed at benefiting laborers. His concern for the well-being of his state and for the workers who keep it growing was evident at a Worker Memorial Day celebration he organized in April 2001. At the gathering, he said,

We [Washington laborers] harvest trees, catch fish, grow crops, build skyscrapers and airplanes, haul huge containers filled with goods produced in the United States and around the world and drive the world's information age

Gary Locke, who in 1996 became the first Chinese American governor in U.S. history, celebrates with his daughter after winning reelection in 2000.

revolution. But there is another side to our success. The work can be dangerous. People get hurt. Some get killed. So we are gathered together today to remember those who have fallen while helping us build this unprecedented prosperity.[81]

In recent years, many people of Chinese descent, like Governor Locke, have served both their state and the federal government in influential positions. As Chinese Americans have earned law degrees, they have been appointed to various state and local courts and as federal judges. They have won elected offices such as the secretary of state in California and the lieutenant governor in Delaware. In 1994, President Clinton appointed March Fong Eu as the U.S. ambassador to Micronesia, and in 2001 President George W. Bush appointed Elaine Chao as the secretary of labor.

Stereotyping

Despite these many successes, even today some people in American society continue to perpetuate a stereotypical image of those of Chinese heritage. By the end of the twentieth century, as the number of students of Asian descent greatly increased on college and university campuses, a new stereotype of Chinese Americans emerged. Newspapers and other media began writing and speaking of the "model minority," grouping all Asians together— including Chinese, Japanese, Filipinos, Koreans, and Vietnamese—and touting their achievements as doctors, professors, scientists, technicians, and mathemati-

cians. Just as they resented past stereotypes, whether good or bad, Chinese Americans are angry with this new stereotyping and its results. They dislike being called "overachievers" or "nerdish." They point out that many Chinese struggle in low-paying jobs or in sweatshops and still long for a better life.

As the media continued to use stereotypes, resentment flared up against the "model minority." Racial slurs and slogans showed up on colleges across the nation during the 1980s and '90s. Anti-Asian graffiti appeared on college dormitory walls and bulletin boards, and discrimination against Asian Americans grew.

Sometimes this prejudice turns to violence. One of the most dramatic incidents occurred in Michigan in 1982 when a young Chinese American named Vincent Chin and two friends went to a Detroit bar to celebrate Chin's upcoming wedding. Two men approached Chin, calling him names. A fight soon started, and Chin ran out of the bar. The two men got a baseball bat from their car trunk and chased him down the street. When they caught him in front of a McDonald's restaurant, they beat him to death. The Asian American community was outraged by the crime and the light punishment given to the two men; they were sentenced to three years' probation. As a result of this incident, the Chinese American community drew close and bonded with other Asians, forming nationwide alliances to work for civil rights and justice for all Asians. One of these groups, the Organization of Chinese America in Washington, D.C., now has branches across the country.

Finding Success

In spite of such actions, Chinese Americans find great pleasure and satisfaction in their awards, elections, accomplishments, and contributions to the United States. Many came as poor immigrants, and they and their children have worked to find a meaningful place in American society. Today they have established museums, educational projects, websites, and cultural organizations to maintain a link with their Chinese heritage and immigrant past. At the same time, they appreciate American customs.

By maintaining strong family ties, however, Chinese Americans have been able to show respect for their heritage, even as they joined the American mainstream. One way they have managed to do this is by keeping their ancient tradition of valuing family life. One immigrant from Hong Kong whose family remained poor told an interviewer, "Most of us are struggling [but] . . . even though life is difficult here we both [she and her husband] have jobs and we have a nice family. So we are still happy."[82]

Another of the values Chinese Americans have clung to in America is the age-old belief in the importance of education. From ancient times, Chinese culture valued scholars and learning. When the early immigrants came, most carried this high regard for education with them. They believed schooling and knowledge would bring a better life in their new country. Today, immigrants continue to work long hours so they or their children can get an education. Wendy Wen-Yan Yen describes how her husband attended college. She says, "My husband found a job in a library as a custodian working from six to ten o'clock in the morning and another job in a nearby Chinese restaurant washing dishes. Having two jobs plus full time schooling, he could hardly see me."[83] But he finally graduated and got a good job.

Although racism and prejudice still exist, Chinese immigrants have been able to overcome obstacles, and through their talents and efforts they have been able to assimilate into American society. During the frontier days, they arrived looking for gold and jobs and discovered a country where they could live and add to the richness of pioneer life. Today, immigrants still come wanting to find jobs and make contributions, and both Chinese Americans and new immigrants continue to affect, enhance, and change the fabric of American life.

N O T E S

Chapter 1: Immigration Begins from Imperial China

1. Quoted in Hamilton Holt, ed., *The Life Stories of Undistinguished Americans as Told by Themselves*. New York: James Pott, 1906, pp. 281–82.
2. Quoted in Holt, *The Life Stories of Undistinguished Americans as Told by Themselves,* pp. 286–87.
3. Kil Young Zo, *Chinese Emigration in the United States, 1850–1880*. New York: Arno Press, 1978, p. 21.
4. John King Fairbanks, *The United States and China*. Cambridge, MA: Harvard University Press, 1983, p. 152.
5. Quoted in Holt, *The Life Stories of Undistinguished Americans as Told by Themselves,* p. 286.
6. Fairbanks, *The United States and China,* p. 163.
7. Liping Zhu, *A Chinaman's Chance: The Chinese on the Rocky Mountain Mining Frontier*. Niwot: University Press of Colorado, 1997, p. 17.
8. Mary Roberts Coolidge, *Chinese Immigration*. New York: Henry Holt, 1909, pp. 16–17.
9. Coolidge, *Chinese Immigration,* p. 17.
10. Betty Lee Sung, *Mountain of Gold: The Story of the Chinese in America*. New York: Macmillan, 1967, pp. 22–23.

Chapter 2: The Journey

11. Quoted in *Chinese Immigration: Testimony Taken Before a Committee of the Senate of the State of California*. Sacramento, CA: State Printing Office, 1876, p. 31.
12. Sung, *Mountain of Gold,* pp. 22–23.
13. Zhu, *A Chinaman's Chance,* p. 24.
14. Sung, *Mountain of Gold,* pp. 23–24.
15. Quoted in Ronald Takaki, *Strangers from a Different Shore*. Boston: Little, Brown, 1998, p. 71.
16. Zo, *Chinese Emigration in the United States, 1850–1880,* p. 110.
17. Quoted in Zhu, *A Chinaman's Chance,* p. 26.
18. Quoted in Zhu, *A Chinaman's Chance,* pp. 27–28.
19. Zhu, *A Chinaman's Chance,* pp. 30–31.
20. Sung, *Mountain of Gold,* pp. 100–101.
21. Angel Island Immigration Station Foundation, "Angel Island: The Pacific Gateway," October 18, 2000. www.ai-isf.org.
22. Quoted in Takaki, *Strangers from a Different Shore,* p. 237.
23. Marlon K. Hom, *Songs of Gold Mountain*. Berkeley: University of California Press, 1987, p. 72.
24. Quoted in Shin-Shan Henry Tsai, *The Chinese Experience in America*. Bloomington: Indiana University Press, 1986, p. 101.

Chapter 3: Finding Work in America

25. Quoted in James Loewen, *The Mississippi Chinese*. Cambridge, MA: Harvard University Press, 1971, p. 24.

26. Quoted in Holt, *The Life Stories of Undistinguished Americans as Told by Themselves,* pp. 291–92.
27. Sucheng Chan, *The Bittersweet Soil.* Los Angeles: University of California Press, 1986, p. 87.
28. Quoted in Stephen E. Ambrose, *Nothing Like It in the World.* New York: Simon and Schuster, 2000, p. 150.
29. Quoted in Ambrose, *Nothing Like It in the World,* p. 156.
30. Quoted in Ambrose, *Nothing Like It in the World,* p. 201.
31. Quoted in *Getting Together,* "Chinese-American Workers: Past and Present," vol. 1, no. 1, 1970, pp. 6–7.
32. Quoted in Ambrose, *Nothing Like It in the World,* p. 164.

Chapter 4: Forming Communities in the West

33. Quoted in Connie Young Yu, "Who Are the Chinese Americans?" in the *Reference Library of Asian America,* vol. 1. Detroit: Gale Research, 1995, p. 44.
34. Sung, *Mountain of Gold,* p. 44.
35. Quoted in Coolidge, *Chinese Immigration,* pp. 438–39.
36. Yu, *The Reference Library of Asian Americans,* p. 50.
37. Jacob A. Riis, *How the Other Half Lives.* Ed. David Leviatin. New York: St. Martin's Press, 1996, p. 120.
38. Quoted in Huping Ling, *Surviving on the Gold Mountain.* New York: State University of New York Press, 1998, p. 69.
39. Quoted in Takaki, *Strangers from a Different Shore,* p. 118.
40. Quoted in Takaki, *Strangers from a Different Shore,* p. 115.

41. Quoted in Ruthanne Lum McCunn, *Chinese American Portraits.* San Francisco: Chronicle Books, 1988, p. 43.
42. Jade Snow Wong, *Fifth Chinese Daughter.* New York: Harper and Brothers, 1945, p. 13.
43. Wong, *Fifth Chinese Daughter,* p. 34.

Chapter 5: Working and Forming Communities in Hawaii

44. Clarence E. Glick, *Sojourners and Settlers.* University Press of Hawaii, 1980, p. 131.
45. Tin-Yuke Char, ed., *The Sandalwood Mountains.* Honolulu: University Press of Hawaii, 1975, p. 41.
46. Quoted in Takaki, *Strangers from a Different Shore,* p. 38.
47. Quoted in Glick, *Sojourners and Settlers,* p. 164.
48. Quoted in William Carlson Smith, *Americans in Process.* New York: Arno Press and the New York Times, 1970, p. 55.
49. Quoted in Char, *The Sandalwood Mountains,* pp. 201–02.
50. Quoted in Glick, *Sojourners and Settlers,* p. 69.
51. Glick, *Sojourners and Settlers,* p. 165.
52. Quoted in Glick, *Sojourners and Settlers,* p. 201.
53. Char, *The Sandalwood Mountains,* p. 147.

Chapter 6: A Turning Point

54. Quoted in K. Scott Wong and Sucheng Chan, eds., *Claiming America.* Philadelphia: Temple University Press, 1998, p. 134.
55. Quoted in Wong and Chan, *Claiming America,* p. 145.

56. Quoted in Victor G. and Brette de Bary Nee, *Longtime Californ'*. New York: Pantheon Books, 1972, p. 154.

57. *Chinese Press*, "First Chinese WAAC: New York's Emily Lee Shek," September 25, 1942.

58. Quoted in Nee, *Longtime Californ'*, pp. 154–55.

59. Quoted in Ronald Takaki, *Double Victory*. Boston: Little, Brown, 2000, p. 116.

60. Quoted in Takaki, *Double Victory*, p. 116.

61. Quoted in Takaki, *Double Victory*, p. 42.

62. Quoted in Gloria Heyung Chun, *Of Orphans and Warriors*. New Brunswick, NJ: Rutgers University Press, 2000, p. 67.

63. Quoted in Ling, *Surviving on the Gold Mountain*, pp. 125–26.

64. Quoted in Nee, *Longtime Californ'*, p. 155.

65. Tung Pok Chin, with Winifred C. Chin, *Paper Son*. Philadelphia: Temple University Press, 2000, p. 86.

Chapter 7: Living in Two Worlds

66. Quoted in Chun, *Of Orphans and Warriors*, p. 41.

67. Char, *The Sandalwood Mountains*, pp. 182–83.

68. Rose Hum Lee, *The Chinese in the United States of America*. Hong Kong: Hong Kong University Press, 1960, p. 279.

69. Zhu, *A Chinaman's Chance*, p. 83.

70. Quoted in Nee, *Longtime Californ'*, p. 152.

71. Wong, *Fifth Chinese Daughter*, pp. 113–14.

72. Wong, *Fifth Chinese Daughter*, pp. 109–10.

73. Quoted in Wong and Chan, *Claiming America*, p. 135.

74. Wong, *Fifth Chinese Daughter*, pp. 108–109.

75. Char, *The Sandalwood Mountains*, p. 134.

76. Chinese Historical and Cultural Project, *Virtual Library Virtual Museum* "Moon Festival," February 27, 2001. www.chcp.org/VMoonfestival.html, p. 3 of 3.

Chapter 8: Changing Patterns

77. Sung, *Mountain of Gold*, p. 150.

78. Quoted in John Koch, "Connie Chung: The Interview," *Boston Globe*, Sunday City Edition Magazine, June 29, 1997, p. 12.

79. Quoted in Lisa Leigh Parney, "Celebrated Cellist Builds a Silk Road," *Christian Science Monitor*, January 7, 2000, p. 19.

80. Quoted in Parney, "Celebrated Cellist Builds a Silk Road," p. 19.

81. Quoted in "Governor Gary Locke's Remarks," April 25, 2001, www.governor.wa.gov/speeches/speechesview.asp?SpeechSeg=278.

82. Quoted in Ling, *Surviving on the Gold Mountain*, p. 161.

83. Quoted in Ling, *Surviving on the Gold Mountain*, p.163.

FOR FURTHER READING

Books

Lani Ah Tye Farkas, *Bury My Bones in America*. Nevada City, CA: Carl Mautz Press, 1998. Farkas recounts the true story of her great-grandfather who came to California in the 1850s. She traces her family through two generations in California and includes family photos and poignant stories.

Peter Kwong, *Forbidden Workers*. New York: New Press, 1997. This book, by a well-known authority on Chinese Americans and the smuggling of humans, is an exposé of the mistreatment of illegal Chinese immigrants who continue to come to the United States. It examines the issues of racial prejudice and the need for cheap labor that allow these immigrants looking for the promised land to be exploited.

Calvin Lee, *Chinatown, USA*. New York: Doubleday, 1965. Interviews of hundreds of people of Chinese descent are used to support the author's description of Chinatowns.

Jodine Mayberry, *Recent American Immigrants: Chinese*. New York: Franklin Watts, 1990. A concise and brief basic history for young adults of Chinese immigration with photographs, charts, and maps. The book is divided into four eras: labor, 1849–1882; exclusion, 1882–1943; limited immigration, 1947–1965; and Asian refugees, 1965–1990.

Dusanka Miscevic and Peter Kwong, *Chinese America: The Immigrant Experience*. Hong Kong: Hugh Lauter Levin Association, 2000. With text, photographs, and illustrations, including posters and early magazine art, this book gives a real flavor of the early years of Chinese immigration. The movie posters of the 1920s and '30s recall the stereotyping of Chinese Americans by Hollywood, but the later photographs show Chinese Americans as they become a part of mainstream American society.

Northwest Institute of Acupuncture and Oriental Medicine, "What Is Oriental Medicine?" 2001. www.niaom.edu. This educational institution answers the most frequently asked questions about Oriental medicine and how it works. It also describes what needs to be done in order to study Oriental medicine at the nonprofit educational institute.

Linda Perrin, *Coming to America: Immigrants from the Far East*. New York: Delacorte Press, 1980. This young adult book covers Asian immigration of the Chinese, Japanese, Filipino, and Vietnamese and contains some photographs representing the East Asian immigrants' lives. There is some comparison between the various groups and their experiences.

Michael Peterson and David Perimutt, *Charlie Two Shoes and the Marines of Love Company*. Annapolis, MD: United States Naval Institute Press, 1999. The story of a young Chinese boy who brings food and firewood to a group of U.S. Marines stationed in northern China at the end of World War II. The Marines promise to bring the boy they call Charlie Two Shoes to the United States when they return home. This book chronicles Charlie's life from his first meeting to fifty years later when Charlie Two Shoes and his family arrive in the United States.

Benson Tong, *The Chinese Americans*. Westport, CT: Greenwood Press, 2000. The author looks at Chinese immigrants from 1780 to the present and how they viewed themselves and their place in American history.

Judy Yung, *Unbound Feet*. Berkeley: University of California Press, 1995. Inspired by the civil rights and women's movements, the author began to look for her historical roots and ended by writing a social history of Chinese women in San Francisco. Using oral history interviews, Yung covers the period from 1902 through World War II.

————, *Unbound Voices*. Berkeley: University of California Press, 1999. Using primary documents as well as recorded interviews, the book lets women tell their own stories. Included are their testimonies as they were interrogated at Angel Island and their poems as lonely wives.

Jianli Zhao, *Strangers in the City*. New York: Garland, 2000. This book is based on interviews with many people who are part of Atlanta, Georgia's Chinese community. It tells of the experiences of Asians in more recent times in an old southern community.

WORKS CONSULTED

Books

Stephen E. Ambrose, *Nothing Like It in the World*. New York: Simon and Schuster, 2000. Describes in detail the building of the transcontinental railroad from 1863 to 1869.

Sucheng Chan, *The Bittersweet Soil*. Los Angeles: University of California Press, 1986. Examines the land leases and other official archives around California, documenting Chinese participation in agriculture from 1860 to 1910.

Tin-Yuke Char, ed., *The Sandalwood Mountains*. Honolulu: University Press of Hawaii, 1975. A wide collection of writings from newspapers to government documents describing the lives of the Chinese in Hawaii in the years before World War II.

Jack Chen, *The Chinese of America*. San Francisco: Harper & Row, 1980. A comprehensive history of the Chinese in the United States by a "new wave" immigrant and scholar.

Tung Pok Chin, with Winifred C. Chin, *Paper Son*. Philadelphia: Temple University Press, 2000. A biography of a "paper son" living in the United States from the Great Depression through the fearful times of the McCarthy era. Tung Pok Chin (whose paper name was Bing Chan) spent nine years writing his memoirs, which his son published posthumously.

Chinese Immigration: Testimony Taken Before a Committee of the Senate of the State of California. Sacramento, CA: State Printing Office, 1876. This well-indexed primary-source document includes the testimony of several prominent citizens on a variety of topics concerning Chinese immigration.

Gloria Heyung Chun, *Of Orphans and Warriors*. Rutgers University Press, 2000. The book looks at the Chinese Americans as they view themselves and their culture and how their identity has changed over time.

Mary Roberts Coolidge, *Chinese Immigration*. New York: Henry Holt, 1909. An anthropologist traces the immigration of Chinese from 1848 until 1906.

John King Fairbanks, *The United States and China*. Cambridge, MA: Harvard University Press, 1983. A renowned China scholar attempts to explain China and its history to American readers.

Clarence E. Glick, *Sojourners and Settlers*. Honolulu: University Press of Hawaii, 1980. Traces the migration of the Chinese into Hawaii and explores the foundation for the multiethnic society.

Hamilton Holt, ed., *The Life Stories of Undistinguished Americans as Told by Themselves*. New York: James Pott, 1906. Various immigrants tell their stories, including Lee Chew's "Life Story of a Chinaman."

Marlon K. Hom, *Songs of Gold Mountain*. Berkeley: University of California Press, 1987. This book looks at the literary development of the Chinese immigrants in California.

Rose Hum Lee, *The Chinese in the United States of America*. Hong Kong:

Hong Kong University Press, 1960. A well-known sociologist describes more than one hundred years of Chinese settlement in the United States.

Huping Ling, *Surviving on the Gold Mountain*. New York: State University of New York Press, 1998. A history with some photographs describing Chinese American women and their lives.

James Loewen, *The Mississippi Chinese.* Cambridge, MA: Harvard University Press, 1971. A sociologist compares the past experiences of Chinese and blacks in Mississippi.

Pardee Lowe, *Father and Glorious Descendant.* Boston: Little, Brown, 1943. A son writes a memoir of his father, an immigrant to the United States who became a U.S. citizen.

Ruthanne Lum McCunn, *Chinese American Portraits.* San Francisco: Chronicle Books, 1988. With many photographs and short accounts, the author presents personal histories of Chinese immigrants from 1828 to 1988.

Victor G. and Brett de Bary Nee, *Longtime Californ'.* New York: Pantheon Books, 1972. Using personal interviews, the book takes a look at San Francisco's Chinatown through the eyes of the people who lived there in the early 1970s.

Dennis Ng, ed., *Origins and Destinations.* Los Angeles: Chinese Historical Society of Southern California, 1994. A joint project of the Chinese Historical Society of Southern California and the UCLA Asian American Studies Center, the book contains forty-one essays on a wide variety of topics about Chinese experiences in America.

Jacob A. Riis, *How the Other Half Lives.* Ed. David Leviatin. New York: St. Martin's Press, 1996. A reissue of the original 1890 "Studies Among the Tenements of New York," with additional uncropped photos and an introduction by the editor.

William Carlson Smith, *Americans in Process.* New York: Arno Press and the New York Times, 1970. This book is part of the American Immigration Collection and was originally published in 1937. It is a study of the second generation of those of Chinese ancestry on the Pacific coast.

Betty Lee Sung, *Mountain of Gold: The Story of the Chinese in America.* New York: Macmillan, 1967. Concerned with the lack of correct information about the early Chinese immigrants, Sung set out to explain their lives in America more accurately.

Ronald Takaki, *A Larger Memory.* Boston: Little, Brown, 1998. A historian of Asian descent uses primary accounts of people of color who lived in the United States.

———, *Double Victory.* Boston: Little, Brown, 2000. Professor Takaki writes a multicultural history of America during World War II.

———, *Strangers from a Different Shore.* Boston: Little, Brown, 1998. In his undated and revised edition, Professor Takaki gives a comprehensive history of Asian Americans' experiences in the United States.

Shin-Shan Henry Tsai, *The Chinese Experience in America.* Bloomington: Indiana University Press, 1986. A scholarly and detailed history of the Chinese in the United States from the 1840s to the 1980s.

Jade Snow Wong, *Fifth Chinese Daughter.* New York: Harper and Brothers, 1945.

This autobiography of the daughter of Chinese immigrants covers the most "significant episodes" of her life in San Francisco's Chinatown through her graduation from college until World War II.

K. Scott Wong and Sucheng Chan, eds., *Claiming America.* Philadelphia: Temple University Press, 1998. With chapters by the editors and other scholars, their book looks at both the immigrant generation and Chinese Americans during the painful exclusion era.

Connie Young Yu, "Who Are the Chinese Americans?" in *The Reference Library of Asian Americans,* vol. 1. Detroit: Gale Research, 1995. A brief history with the highlights of the Chinese Americans and their experiences on the mainland.

Liping Zhu, *A Chinaman's Chance: The Chinese on the Rocky Mountain Mining Frontier.* University Press of Colorado, 1997. A wonderfully descriptive history of the Chinese living and mining on the Rocky Mountain frontier.

Kil Young Zo, *Chinese Emigration in the United States, 1850–1880.* New York: Arno Press, 1978. An American Chinese scholar describes the early years of Chinese immigration, using primary documents in both English and Chinese.

Periodicals

Chinese Press, "First Chinese WAAC: New York's Emily Lee Shek," September 25, 1942. This article explains Emily Lee Shek's attempts to sign up and show her patriotism for her country.

Getting Together, "Chinese-American Workers: Past and Present," vol. 1, no. 1, 1970. A section of the article describes the construction of the Central Pacific Railroad.

John Koch, "Connie Chung: The Interview," *Boston Globe,* Sunday City Edition Magazine, June 29, 1997. This interview with Connie Chung discusses her personal life, including her desire to please her father as a son would and make the Chung name famous.

Lisa Leigh Parney, "Celebrated Cellist Builds a Silk Road," *Christian Science Monitor,* January 7, 2000. This is an interview with Yo-Yo Ma; he explains his Silk Road Project and his goals for its future.

Websites

Angel Island Immigration Station Foundation (www.aiisf.org). Describes the history of Angel Island and its present-day operations. www.aiisf.org.

Chinese Historical and Cultural Project, (www.chcp.org). A good source for a variety of topics concerning the history of the Chinese in California.

Governor Gary Locke, (www.governor. wa.gov). The governor's website explains his actions and policies in office.

House of Representatives, Office of Congressman David Wu, Oregon, First District (www.house.gov/wu). A site detailing Congressman Wu's activities and positions.

Instructional Technology Project, "Chinese American History" (www.itp.berkeley. edu). This site contains an excellent timeline with links to more information about the events listed.

INDEX

PICTURE CREDITS

ABOUT THE AUTHOR

Barbara Lee Bloom grew up in California and graduated from UCLA. She received an M.A. from California State University, at Long Beach, and a doctorate from the University of Vermont. She lives in Vermont and teaches history at Champlain College. She has written biography and historical fiction for young people, and her work has been published in the United States and Australia.

DELETED

FROM COLLECTION